HMH SCIENCE DIMENSIONS™
SPACE SCIENCE

Module H

This Write-In Book belongs to

Sarah Quevedo

Teacher/Room

Garvey / 201

Houghton Mifflin Harcourt™

Consulting Authors

Michael A. DiSpezio

Global Educator
North Falmouth,
Massachusetts

Michael DiSpezio has authored many HMH instructional programs for Science and Mathematics. He has also authored numerous trade books and multimedia programs on various topics and hosted dozens of studio and location broadcasts for various organizations in the United States and worldwide. Most recently, he has been working with educators to provide strategies for implementing the Next Generation Science Standards, particularly the Science and Engineering Practices, Crosscutting Concepts, and the use of Evidence Notebooks. To all his projects, he brings his extensive background in science, his expertise in classroom teaching at the elementary, middle, and high school levels, and his deep experience in producing interactive and engaging instructional materials.

Marjorie Frank

Science Writer and Content-Area Reading Specialist
Brooklyn, New York

An educator and linguist by training, a writer and poet by nature, Marjorie Frank has authored and designed a generation of instructional materials in all subject areas, including past HMH Science programs. Her other credits include authoring science issues of an award-winning children's magazine, writing game-based digital assessments, developing blended learning materials for young children, and serving as instructional designer and coauthor of pioneering school-to-work software. In addition, she has served on the adjunct faculty of Hunter, Manhattan, and Brooklyn Colleges, teaching courses in science methods, literacy, and writing. For *HMH Science Dimensions™*, she has guided the development of our K–2 strands and our approach to making connections between NGSS and Common Core ELA/literacy standards.

Acknowledgments for Covers

Cover credits: (telescope) ©HMH; (Mars) ©Stocktrek Images, Inc./Alamy.

Section Header Master Art: (rivers on top of Greenland Ice Sheet) © Maria-Jose Viñas, NASA Earth Science News Team.

Copyright © 2018 by Houghton Mifflin Harcourt Publishing Company

Printed in the U.S.A.

ISBN   978-0-544-86101-5

13 0928 25 24 23 22

4500844125   C D E F G

Michael R. Heithaus, PhD

Dean, College of Arts, Sciences & Education Professor, Department of Biological Sciences Florida International University Miami, Florida

Mike Heithaus joined the FIU Biology Department in 2003 and has served as Director of the Marine Sciences Program and Executive Director of the School of Environment, Arts, and Society, which brings together the natural and social sciences and humanities to develop solutions to today's environmental challenges. He now serves as Dean of the College of Arts, Sciences & Education. His research focuses on predator-prey interactions and the ecological importance of large marine species. He has helped to guide the development of Life Science content in *HMH Science Dimensions™*, with a focus on strategies for teaching challenging content as well as the science and engineering practices of analyzing data and using computational thinking.

Cary I. Sneider, PhD

Associate Research Professor Portland State University Portland, Oregon

While studying astrophysics at Harvard, Cary Sneider volunteered to teach in an Upward Bound program and discovered his real calling as a science teacher. After teaching middle and high school science in Maine, California, Costa Rica, and Micronesia, he settled for nearly three decades at Lawrence Hall of Science in Berkeley, California, where he developed skills in curriculum development and teacher education. Over his career, Cary directed more than 20 federal, state, and foundation grant projects and was a writing team leader for the Next Generation Science Standards. He has been instrumental in ensuring *HMH Science Dimensions™* meets the high expectations of the NGSS and provides an effective three-dimensional learning experience for all students.

Program Advisors

Paul D. Asimow, PhD
Eleanor and John R. McMillan Professor of Geology and Geochemistry
California Institute of Technology
Pasadena, California

Joanne Bourgeois
Professor Emerita
Earth & Space Sciences
University of Washington
Seattle, WA

Dr. Eileen Cashman
Professor
Humboldt State University
Arcata, California

Elizabeth A. De Stasio, PhD
Raymond J. Herzog Professor of Science
Lawrence University
Appleton, Wisconsin

Perry Donham, PhD
Lecturer
Boston University
Boston, Massachusetts

Shila Garg, PhD
Emerita Professor of Physics
Former Dean of Faculty & Provost
The College of Wooster
Wooster, Ohio

Tatiana A. Krivosheev, PhD
Professor of Physics
Clayton State University
Morrow, Georgia

Mark B. Moldwin, PhD
Professor of Space Sciences and Engineering
University of Michigan
Ann Arbor, Michigan

Ross H. Nehm
Stony Brook University (SUNY)
Stony Brook, NY

Kelly Y. Neiles, PhD
Assistant Professor of Chemistry
St. Mary's College of Maryland
St. Mary's City, Maryland

John Nielsen-Gammon, PhD
Regents Professor
Department of Atmospheric Sciences
Texas A&M University
College Station, Texas

Dr. Sten Odenwald
Astronomer
NASA Goddard Spaceflight Center
Greenbelt, Maryland

Bruce W. Schafer
Executive Director
Oregon Robotics Tournament & Outreach Program
Beaverton, Oregon

Barry A. Van Deman
President and CEO
Museum of Life and Science
Durham, North Carolina

Kim Withers, PhD
Assistant Professor
Texas A&M University-Corpus Christi
Corpus Christi, Texas

Adam D. Woods, PhD
Professor
California State University, Fullerton
Fullerton, California

Classroom Reviewers

Cynthia Book, PhD
John Barrett Middle School
Carmichael, California

Katherine Carter, MEd
Fremont Unified School District
Fremont, California

Theresa Hollenbeck, MEd
Winston Churchill Middle School
Carmichael, California

Kathryn S. King
Science and AVID Teacher
Norwood Jr. High School
Sacramento, California

Donna Lee
Science/STEM Teacher
Junction Ave. K8
Livermore, California

Rebecca S. Lewis
Science Teacher
North Rockford Middle School
Rockford, Michigan

Bryce McCourt
8th Grade Science Teacher/Middle School Curriculum Chair
Cudahy Middle School
Cudahy, Wisconsin

Sarah Mrozinski
Teacher
St. Sebastian School
Milwaukee, Wisconsin

Raymond Pietersen
Science Program Specialist
Elk Grove Unified School District
Elk Grove, California

You are a scientist!
You are naturally curious.

Have you ever wondered . . .

- why is it difficult to catch a fly?
- how a new island can appear in an ocean?
- how to design a great tree house?
- how a spacecraft can send messages across the solar system?

HMH SCIENCE DIMENSIONS™
will *SPARK* your curiosity!

AND prepare you for

✓	tomorrow
✓	next year
✓	college or career
✓	life!

Where do you see yourself in 15 years?

Observe

Collect Data

Be a scientist.
Work like real scientists work.

Analyze

Images/Corbis

Be an engineer.

Solve problems like engineers do.

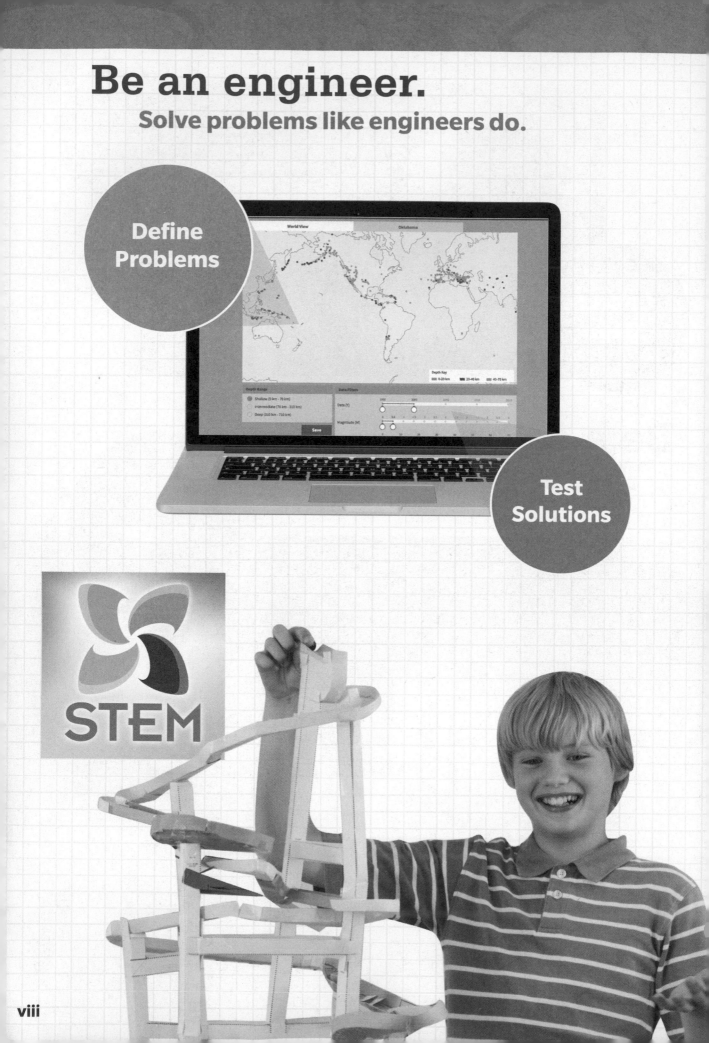

Define Problems

Test Solutions

STEM

Gather Information

Think Critically

Explain your world.
Start by asking questions.

Conduct Investigations

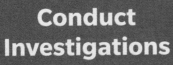

Collaborate

Develop Explanations

Construct Arguments

There's more than one way to the answer. What's YOURS?

YOUR Program

Write-In Book:

- a brand-new and innovative textbook that will guide you through your next generation curriculum, including your hands-on lab program

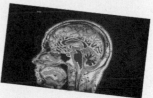

Interactive Online Student Edition:

- a complete online version of your textbook enriched with videos, interactivities, animations, simulations, and room to enter data, draw, and store your work

More tools are available online to help you practice and learn science, including:

- Hands-On Labs
- Science and Engineering Practices Handbook
- Crosscutting Concepts Handbook
- English Language Arts Handbook
- Math Handbook

Contents

UNIT 1

Patterns in the Solar System

Although the sun is far away in space, it lights up Earth.

UNIT 2

57

The Solar System and Universe

The Milky Way can only be seen in a very clear and dark sky and appears as a hazy band of clouds and stars.

Whether you are in the lab or in the field, you are responsible for your own safety and the safety of others. To fulfill these responsibilities and avoid accidents, be aware of the safety of your classmates as well as your own safety at all times. Take your lab work and fieldwork seriously, and behave appropriately. Elements of safety to keep in mind are shown below and on the following pages.

Safety in the Lab

- ☐ Be sure you understand the materials, your procedure, and the safety rules before you start an investigation in the lab.

- ☐ Know where to find and how to use fire extinguishers, eyewash stations, shower stations, and emergency power shutoffs.

- ☐ Use proper safety equipment. Always wear personal protective equipment, such as eye protection and gloves, when setting up labs, during labs, and when cleaning up.

- ☐ Do not begin until your teacher has told you to start. Follow directions.

- ☐ Keep the lab neat and uncluttered. Clean up when you are finished. Report all spills to your teacher immediately. Watch for slip/fall and trip/fall hazards.

- ☐ If you or another student are injured in any way, tell your teacher immediately, even if the injury seems minor.

- ☐ Do not take any food or drink into the lab. Never take any chemicals out of the lab.

Safety in the Field

- ☐ Be sure you understand the goal of your fieldwork and the proper way to carry out the investigation before you begin fieldwork.

- ☐ Use proper safety equipment and personal protective equipment, such as eye protection, that suits the terrain and the weather.

- ☐ Follow directions, including appropriate safety procedures as provided by your teacher.

- ☐ Do not approach or touch wild animals. Do not touch plants unless instructed by your teacher to do so. Leave natural areas as you found them.

- ☐ Stay with your group.

- ☐ Use proper accident procedures, and let your teacher know about a hazard in the environment or an accident immediately, even if the hazard or accident seems minor.

Safety Symbols

To highlight specific types of precautions, the following symbols are used throughout the lab program. Remember that no matter what safety symbols you see within each lab, all safety rules should be followed at all times.

Dress Code

- Wear safety goggles (or safety glasses as appropriate for the activity) at all times in the lab as directed. If chemicals get into your eye, flush your eyes immediately for a minimum of 15 minutes.
- Do not wear contact lenses in the lab.
- Do not look directly at the sun or any intense light source or laser.
- Wear appropriate protective non-latex gloves as directed.
- Wear an apron or lab coat at all times in the lab as directed.
- Tie back long hair, secure loose clothing, and remove loose jewelry. Remove acrylic nails when working with active flames.
- Do not wear open-toed shoes, sandals, or canvas shoes in the lab.

Glassware and Sharp Object Safety

- Do not use chipped or cracked glassware.
- Use heat-resistant glassware for heating or storing hot materials.
- Notify your teacher immediately if a piece of glass breaks.
- Use extreme care when handling any sharp or pointed instruments.
- Do not cut an object while holding the object unsupported in your hands. Place the object on a suitable cutting surface, and always cut in a direction away from your body.

Chemical Safety

- If a chemical gets on your skin, on your clothing, or in your eyes, rinse it immediately for a minimum of 15 minutes (using the shower, faucet, or eyewash station), and alert your teacher.
- Do not clean up spilled chemicals unless your teacher directs you to do so.
- Do not inhale any gas or vapor unless directed to do so by your teacher. If you are instructed to note the odor of a substance, wave the fumes toward your nose with your hand. This is called wafting. Never put your nose close to the source of the odor.
- Handle materials that emit vapors or gases in a well-ventilated area.
- Keep your hands away from your face while you are working on any activity.

Safety Symbols, continued

Electrical Safety

- Do not use equipment with frayed electrical cords or loose plugs.
- Do not use electrical equipment near water or when clothing or hands are wet.
- Hold the plug housing when you plug in or unplug equipment. Do not pull on the cord.
- Use only GFI-protected electrical receptacles.

Heating and Fire Safety

- Be aware of any source of flames, sparks, or heat (such as flames, heating coils, or hot plates) before working with any flammable substances.
- Know the location of the lab's fire extinguisher and fire-safety blankets.
- Know your school's fire-evacuation routes.
- If your clothing catches on fire, walk to the lab shower to put out the fire. Do not run.
- Never leave a hot plate unattended while it is turned on or while it is cooling.
- Use tongs or appropriately insulated holders when handling heated objects.
- Allow all equipment to cool before storing it.

Plant and Animal Safety

- Do not eat any part of a plant.
- Do not pick any wild plant unless your teacher instructs you to do so.
- Handle animals only as your teacher directs.
- Treat animals carefully and respectfully.
- Wash your hands throughly with soap and water after handling any plant or animal.

Cleanup

- Clean all work surfaces and protective equipment as directed by your teacher.
- Dispose of hazardous materials or sharp objects only as directed by your teacher.
- Wash your hands throughly with soap and water before you leave the lab or after any activity.

Student Safety Quiz

Circle the letter of the BEST answer.

1. Before starting an investigation or lab procedure, you should
   A. try an experiment of your own
   B. open all containers and packages
   C. read all directions and make sure you understand them
   D. handle all the equipment to become familiar with it

2. At the end of any activity you should
   A. wash your hands thoroughly with soap and water before leaving the lab
   B. cover your face with your hands
   C. put on your safety goggles
   D. leave hot plates switched on

3. If you get hurt or injured in any way, you should
   A. tell your teacher immediately
   B. find bandages or a first aid kit
   C. go to your principal's office
   D. get help after you finish the lab

4. If your glassware is chipped or broken, you should
   A. use it only for solid materials
   B. give it to your teacher for recycling or disposal
   C. put it back into the storage cabinet
   D. increase the damage so that it is obvious

5. If you have unused chemicals after finishing a procedure, you should
   A. pour them down a sink or drain
   B. mix them all together in a bucket
   C. put them back into their original containers
   D. dispose of them as directed by your teacher

6. If electrical equipment has a frayed cord, you should
   A. unplug the equipment by pulling the cord
   B. let the cord hang over the side of a counter or table
   C. tell your teacher about the problem immediately
   D. wrap tape around the cord to repair it

7. If you need to determine the odor of a chemical or a solution, you should
   A. use your hand to bring fumes from the container to your nose
   B. bring the container under your nose and inhale deeply
   C. tell your teacher immediately
   D. use odor-sensing equipment

8. When working with materials that might fly into the air and hurt someone's eye, you should wear
   A. goggles
   B. an apron
   C. gloves
   D. a hat

9. Before doing experiments involving a heat source, you should know the location of the
   A. door
   B. window
   C. fire extinguisher
   D. overhead lights

10. If you get chemicals in your eye you should
    A. wash your hands immediately
    B. put the lid back on the chemical container
    C. wait to see if your eye becomes irritated
    D. use the eyewash station right away, for a minimum of 15 minutes

Go online to view the Lab Safety Handbook for additional information.

Patterns in the Solar System

This shadow on Earth was cast during a solar eclipse in 1999. During a solar eclipse, the moon moves directly between Earth and the sun, blocking the light from the sun and casting a shadow on Earth.

On Earth we experience many different patterns caused by Earth's position relative to the sun and moon. Some of these patterns are visible in the sky. Others we feel on our skin on a daily basis. In this unit, you will discover the effects of the Earth-sun-moon system on your daily life.

Why It Matters

Here are some questions to consider as you work through the unit. Can you answer any of the questions now? Revisit these questions at the end of the unit to apply what you discovered.

Questions	Notes
What causes seasons?	
Why does the moon's shape and brightness appear to change?	
What causes eclipses?	
How is a new moon the same as or different from a total lunar eclipse?	
How does the sun affect weather and climate?	
How does the Earth-sun-moon system affect life on Earth?	

Unit Starter: Identifying Patterns in Data

This graph represents typical average monthly temperatures for a location at about 45° north latitude in North America. Review these data and answer the following questions.

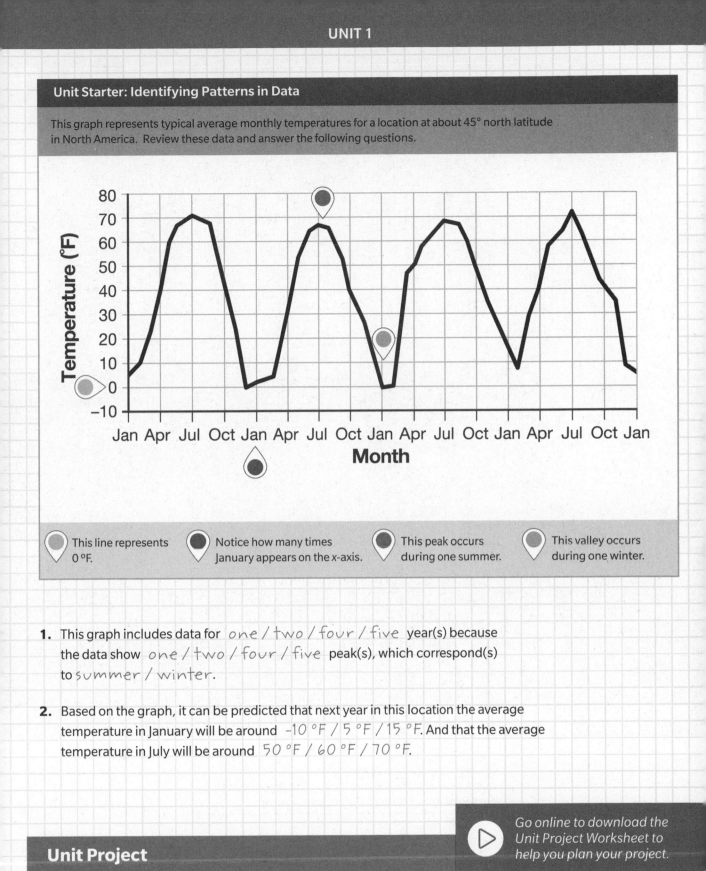

- This line represents 0 °F.
- Notice how many times January appears on the x-axis.
- This peak occurs during one summer.
- This valley occurs during one winter.

1. This graph includes data for one / two / four / five year(s) because the data show one / two / four / five peak(s), which correspond(s) to summer / winter.

2. Based on the graph, it can be predicted that next year in this location the average temperature in January will be around −10 °F / 5 °F / 15 °F. And that the average temperature in July will be around 50 °F / 60 °F / 70 °F.

Go online to download the Unit Project Worksheet to help you plan your project.

Unit Project

Investigate Eclipses in Your Area

When will the next solar or lunar eclipse happen in your area? Will it be a full or partial eclipse? Research information about an upcoming lunar or solar eclipse to plan an eclipse-viewing event for your community.

The Earth-Sun-Moon System

The moon sometimes appears orange as it rises. When the moon is near the horizon, the bending of light in the atmosphere can also distort the moon's shape.

By the end of this lesson . . .

you will be able to explain patterns of the sun, moon, and stars as seen from Earth, monthly patterns of the moon, and eclipses.

CAN YOU EXPLAIN IT?

Why can we see the moon at night and also during the day?

At night, the moon is the biggest, brightest object in the sky. If you look closely, you may also be able to see the moon during the day when the sun is also out.

1. How is the moon similar and different in the two photos?

2. Do you think the shape of the moon would appear to be different if photos were taken a few hours later than the photos shown here? If yes, how would its appearance change?

3. Do you think the shape of the moon would appear to be different if photos were taken one week later than the photos shown here? If yes, how would its appearance change?

EVIDENCE NOTEBOOK As you explore the lesson, gather evidence to help explain why we see the moon at night and also during the day.

Analyzing Daily Patterns in the Sky

You might think of day as the time when you are in school and night as the time when you are home with your family. Or you may think of day as the time when you are awake and night as the time when you are asleep. But the scientific meanings of day and night do not depend on our daily activities.

4. Look at the photo of the sun and Earth. Why is part of Earth light and part of Earth dark?

Although the sun is far away in space, it lights up Earth.

The Sun's Path in the Sky

The sun is always giving off light that reaches Earth. Yet, you experience a daily cycle of light and darkness. The period of time when the sun is directly shining on an area of Earth is daytime. Nighttime is when the sun is not shining directly on an area. The length of daytime and nighttime varies depending on where you are on Earth and the time of year. However, the periods of daytime and nighttime always add up to 24 hours a day on Earth.

During the day, the sun appears to travel across the sky. If you wake up early enough, you can watch the sun rise on the eastern horizon. In the evening, you look to the west to see the sun set on the western horizon. The sun always follows an arc from east to west across the sky. It is highest at noon, but that does not mean it is directly overhead. In the Northern Hemisphere, you can see the sun follow an arc through the southern half of the sky.

Explore ONLINE!

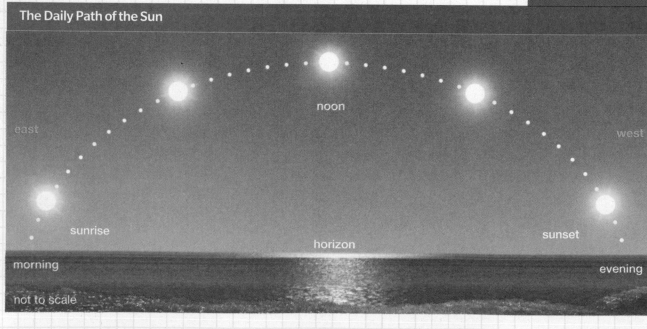

The Daily Path of the Sun

noon

east

west

sunrise

sunset

horizon

morning

evening

not to scale

The Stars' Path in the Sky

Stars shine day and night, but you can only see them after the sun sets. Much like the sun during the day, the stars appear to move east to west during the night. Groups of stars in specific patterns, such as Orion, are called *constellations*. They move through the sky during the night, but they do not change shape or size because the distance between any two stars stays the same. That means you always look for the same pattern of stars to find Orion.

The streaks in this time-lapse photo are made as stars move across the sky during the night.

5. Why do you think we see the stars at nighttime and the sun during daytime?

The Moon's Path in the Sky

After sunset, you might look east for the rising moon. But it is not there. Why is it not there? The moon always rises along the eastern horizon, appears to travel across the sky, and sets along the western horizon a few hours later. But the moon rises at different times during the month, in a regular pattern. Sometimes you can see it in the daytime and sometimes at night. When there are no clouds but you cannot see the moon, it is somewhere on the far side of Earth, below your horizon.

This time-lapse photo shows the moon rising. The sun, stars, and the moon move from east to west across the sky.

6. On one clear night, the moon is high in the sky when the sun sets. It is no longer visible after 11 p.m. Which describes the motion of the moon on this day? Circle all that apply.

    A. The moon traveled from east to west.

    B. The moon rose after the sun set.

    C. The moon set before 11 p.m.

    D. The moon rose during the daytime.

Hands-On Lab
Model the Apparent Motion of the Sun

You will model the Earth-sun system to develop an explanation for night and day and the apparent motion of the sun in the sky.

Procedure

STEP 1 **Act** Work with a partner. Choose who will play the part of the sun and who will play Earth. Write *sun* on one piece of paper and *Earth* on another, and tape the labels to each actor. Stand facing each other. Discuss how the motion of the sun or Earth can result in periods of daytime and nighttime on Earth.

STEP 2 **Act** If you are the actor playing Earth, stand facing the sun. Slowly turn in a circle toward your left. Keep your head in line with your body. Your head is representing Earth. Say *night* when you can no longer see the sun and say *day* when you first see the sun again. Take turns being Earth and the sun. NOTE: Turning toward the left models Earth's counterclockwise movement as you are looking down at the North Pole.

STEP 3 Now use the lamp and foam ball to make a model that explains day and night. Write *Earth* on the tape and put the label around the center of the ball. Hold the ball in front of the lamp and turn the stick toward the left.

Analysis

STEP 4 When I was playing Earth and could see the sun, my face represented the part of Earth that was experiencing day / night.

When I could not see the sun, it was day / night.

When I first saw the sun, it was sunrise / sunset.

When I last saw the sun, it was sunrise / sunset.

It was morning / noon / midnight when I was directly facing the sun.

STEP 5 Think about a compass. If you are facing south, your right shoulder is west and your left shoulder is east. In what direction did you first see the sun in the morning? As you turned, in what direction did the sun seem to move throughout the day?

STEP 6 Based on your observations, why does the sun appear to move across the sky?

Earth's Rotation

When you spin around in one place, you are modeling Earth's rotation. Earth rotates around an imaginary axis running through the North and South Poles. Since you are on Earth, you do not feel it turning, but you experience the rotation in other ways.

Earth's Rotation Explains the Path of the Sun

The apparent motion of the sun, including daytime and nighttime, is caused by Earth's rotation. A day on Earth is 24 hours because Earth completes one full rotation during that time. As Earth spins, different parts of Earth face the sun. It is daytime when an area faces toward the sun and nighttime when it faces away from the sun.

If you were looking down on Earth from the North Pole, it would rotate counterclockwise. Therefore, on Earth, the eastern horizon turns toward the sun first in the morning. Throughout the day, the sun appears to move from east to west as Earth rotates. The sun sets below the western horizon because that is the last area to receive sunlight. The way the sun appears to move always follows the same pattern, rising in the east, moving in an arc across the sky from east to west, and setting in the west.

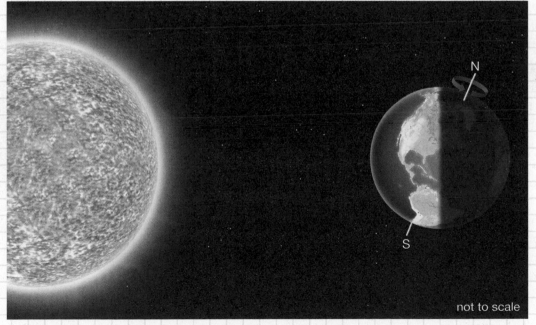

Different parts of Earth face the sun during a 24-hour day because Earth rotates.

not to scale

7. How does the daily cycle of daytime and nighttime depend on Earth's rotation?

A. The sun rises in the west and sets in the east because Earth rotates west to east.

B. It is morning on the part of Earth that is turning into the sun and evening on the part that is turning away from the sun.

C. The Northern Hemisphere experiences daytime while the Southern Hemisphere experiences nighttime because Earth rotates around its axis.

Earth's Rotation Explains the Path of the Stars

During the daytime, the sun is so bright that you cannot see other stars. Look at the diagram. The area of Earth that is experiencing nighttime faces away from the sun, so you are able to see the stars. As with the sun, the stars appear to move from east to west as Earth rotates. Throughout the night, different stars rise and set. The stars rise and become visible over the horizon as Earth rotates. For example, the constellation Orion comes into view in the eastern night sky around 9 p.m. in late November in the Northern Hemisphere. As Earth spins, Orion appears to move westward. Orion is at its highest point in the sky around midnight. Then Orion continues toward the west, where it sets.

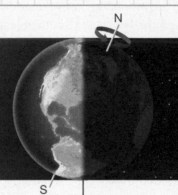

not to scale

S
day side | night side
of Earth | of Earth

Stars are visible at night on the side of Earth facing away from the sun.

8. Stars appear to move because the Earth spins toward the *east / west*. People who live in the eastern United States see *the same / different* stars in the night sky as those who live in the western United States.

Earth's Rotation Explains the Path of the Moon

The moon also appears to move east to west in the sky as Earth rotates. However, the motion of the moon is a bit different than the motion of the sun and the stars because the moon orbits Earth. An **orbit** is the path that a body follows as it travels around another body in space. The moon circles around Earth in the same direction that Earth rotates—counterclockwise when looking down on the North Pole. The moon completes an orbit in 27.3 days, or about one month. Earth rotates much faster than the moon circles Earth. So, the moon's daily pattern of motion from east to west is mainly caused by Earth's rotation. The moon's orbit causes it to rise and set at different times of the day. The moon also appears to slowly move eastward with respect to the background of stars.

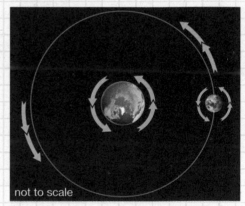

not to scale

The moon orbits Earth in the same direction that Earth rotates.

9. **Discuss** Why are the patterns of movement of the sun, stars, and the moon across Earth's sky similar?

EVIDENCE NOTEBOOK

10. How does the orbit of the moon help to explain why we can see the moon in the sky both during the day and at night? Record your evidence.

The Earth and Moon Move around the Sun

In addition to the fact that the stars appear to move across the sky every night, their rising times change throughout the course of the year. Stars seen from one location during one time of year may not be seen from that same location at a different time of year.

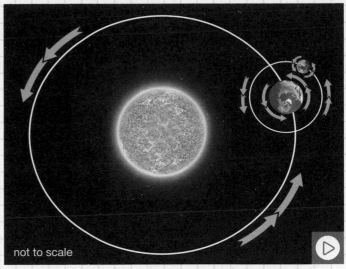

not to scale

Earth completes one orbit around the sun in 365.25 days. The moon travels with Earth around the sun because it orbits Earth.

11. Use the Earth-sun-moon model. Which statements are true about the stars? Circle all that apply.

   A. On a given day, you will only be able to see the stars that are in the opposite direction of the sun.

   B. At opposite sides of Earth's orbit around the sun, a person at the same location on Earth would see the same stars in the night sky.

   C. The different rising times of constellations in the night sky during the year provide evidence that Earth moves around the sun.

Earth orbits the sun and the moon orbits Earth. Earth brings the moon with it as it moves around the sun. One year is the time it takes for Earth to complete one revolution around the sun. In that time, Earth rotates on its axis 365.25 times, so there are 365.25 days in a year. And the moon goes through a full cycle of phases about 12 times in a year.

Do the Math
Analyze Star Motion

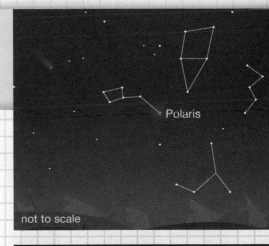

Polaris

not to scale

12. Polaris is also called the *North Star* because Earth's North Pole points toward it. As Earth rotates, other stars seem to spin around Polaris in a counterclockwise direction. In one day, the stars will make one complete circle (360°) around Polaris. Compare the positions of the constellations in the two diagrams. Calculate how many hours have passed between the first and second diagrams.

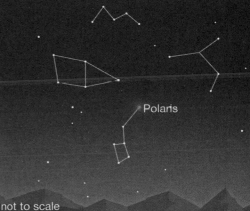

Polaris

not to scale

Analyzing Moon Phases

The moon is the brightest body in the night sky as seen from Earth. But it does not emit any light of its own. The light we see from the moon is light reflected from the sun. The sun always lights half of the moon, and the other half is always dark. As the moon rotates, the areas that are lit by the sun change. Light from the sun falls on Earth in the same way.

The half of the moon facing the sun is lit. The other half is dark because the moon itself is not a source of light. It only reflects light from the sun.

13. Discuss Does the fraction of the moon that receives sunlight ever change? Explain your reasoning.

No, It rotates teo Slowly

Phases of the Moon

You know that the moon appears to move through the sky. It also appears to change shape. It changes from no moon at all, to a small crescent, to a full disc, and back to no moon. These changes are phases of the moon. A **phase** is the change in the sunlit area of one celestial body, such as the moon, as seen from another celestial body, such as Earth. You can predict the phase of the moon on any day because the phases happen in a regular pattern.

The phase that the moon is in on a given day is the same during the day and night, and then is just a little different the next day and night. The side of the moon that is lit is always the side closest to where the sun set. Each night as the crescent grows larger, the moon is seen higher in the sky. As the moon phase continues to grow, the moon is seen farther and farther away from where the sun set. When the moon is full, it rises at just about the time of sunset.

The moon goes through phases during which it appears to change shape.

14. Why does the moon appear to change shape throughout each month?

  A. The fraction of the moon that is lit by the sun changes.

  B. Different parts of the moon become visible from Earth as the moon rotates.

  C. Different parts of the sunlit area are visible from Earth due to motions in the Earth-sun-moon system.

Hands-On Lab
Model Moon Phases

You will model the Earth-sun-moon system to develop an explanation for the changing appearance of the moon as seen from Earth.

MATERIALS
- ball, styrene, on a stick
- lamp with removable shade
- markers
- tape

Procedure

STEP 1 Continue working with your partner. The lamp (sun) should be placed at eye level. Use the marker and tape to label the polystyrene ball as *moon*.

STEP 2 **Act** Have the person playing Earth face the sun (the lamp). The other partner stands next to the sun, facing Earth. Earth holds the moon at arm's length so the moon is between Earth and the sun, then raises the moon so that the moon is slightly higher than his or her head. Record your observations of how much of the moon appears to be lit. Each partner records their observations in the appropriate column of the table.

STEP 3 **Act** Keeping the moon held in the same position at arm's length, Earth will slowly turn in a circle toward the left, stopping at each quarter turn. At each stop, the partners each record their observations of how much of the moon appears to be lit.

STEP 4 **Act** Switch roles and repeat STEPS 2 and 3, completing the table by recording your observations from the other perspective, either as Earth or next to the sun.

Orientation of Earth	Appearance of the moon from Earth	Appearance of the moon from the sun
Facing the sun		
1st quarter turn		
2nd quarter turn (facing away from the sun)		
3rd quarter turn		

Analysis

STEP 5 What is being modeled by the ball when the person playing Earth is turning in a circle?

    A. Earth's rotation

    B. the moon's rotation

    C. Earth's orbit around the sun

    D. the moon's orbit around Earth

STEP 6 When I was playing Earth, the shape of the area that was lit on the moon changed / *stayed the same.*

    When I was facing the sun, the moon appeared to be completely *dark* / lit.

    When I was facing away from the sun, the moon appeared to be completely dark / *lit.*

    When I was observing the moon from the sun, the fraction of the moon that was lit changed / *was always one half.*

STEP 7 **Language SmArts** Compare the information that you have read so far in the text with what you observed in the experiment. Write an explanation for why the phases of the moon occur. Give examples from the model to support your explanation.

Types of Moon Phases

The appearance of the moon as seen from Earth changes as the moon orbits Earth. This happens because observers on Earth see different ratios of light to dark on the moon's surface. Think about what happens when the moon is between Earth and the sun. From Earth, the moon appears totally dark. This is called the new moon. As the moon moves through its orbit, the size of the sunlit part of the moon that you can see from Earth increases. The full moon occurs when Earth is between the moon and the sun. During a full moon, you can see the entire sunlit portion of the moon. As the moon moves farther in its orbit, the lit part of the moon you can see begins to decrease.

    The pattern of surface features that you see on the surface of the moon is the same in any phase. The same side of the moon always faces Earth because the moon's orbit and the time the moon takes to rotate are the same. They are both about 27 days. The moon takes slightly longer—29.5 days—to complete one cycle of phases. This takes longer than 27 days because Earth is also moving in its orbit around the sun. Because Earth and the moon have changed position with respect to the sun, the moon must travel a little longer than 27 days to complete one cycle of phases.

Phases of the Moon

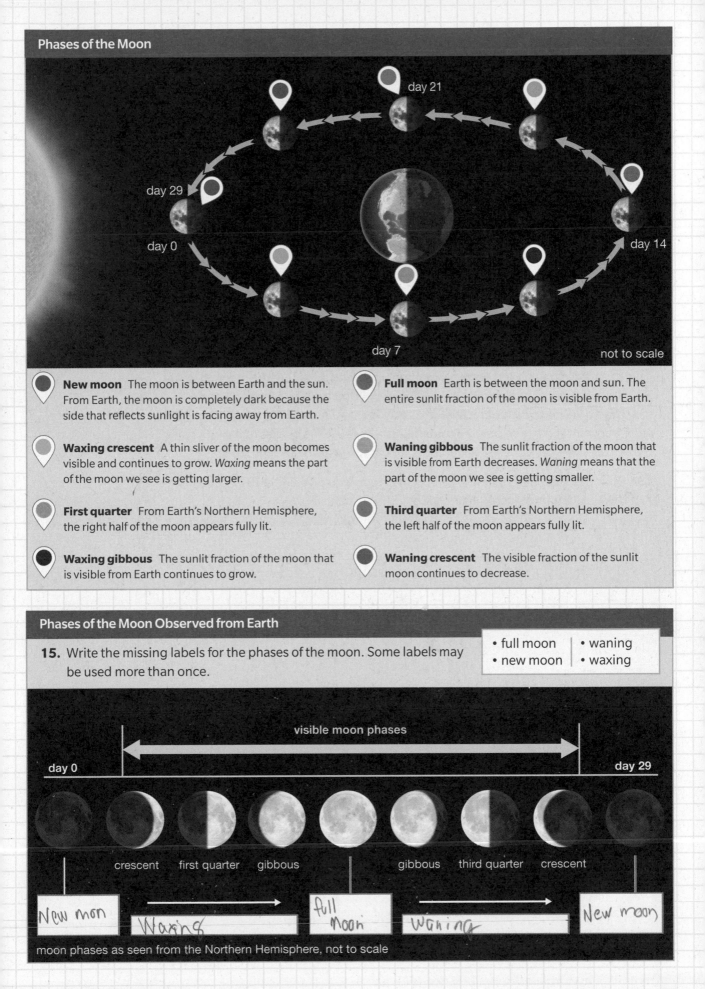

day 21

day 29

day 0

day 14

day 7

not to scale

New moon The moon is between Earth and the sun. From Earth, the moon is completely dark because the side that reflects sunlight is facing away from Earth.

Waxing crescent A thin sliver of the moon becomes visible and continues to grow. *Waxing* means the part of the moon we see is getting larger.

First quarter From Earth's Northern Hemisphere, the right half of the moon appears fully lit.

Waxing gibbous The sunlit fraction of the moon that is visible from Earth continues to grow.

Full moon Earth is between the moon and sun. The entire sunlit fraction of the moon is visible from Earth.

Waning gibbous The sunlit fraction of the moon that is visible from Earth decreases. *Waning* means that the part of the moon we see is getting smaller.

Third quarter From Earth's Northern Hemisphere, the left half of the moon appears fully lit.

Waning crescent The visible fraction of the sunlit moon continues to decrease.

Phases of the Moon Observed from Earth

15. Write the missing labels for the phases of the moon. Some labels may be used more than once.

- full moon
- new moon
- waning
- waxing

visible moon phases

day 0

day 29

crescent   first quarter   gibbous   gibbous   third quarter   crescent

New mon | Waxing | full moon | Waning | New moon

moon phases as seen from the Northern Hemisphere, not to scale

16. During a (full)/ new moon, Earth is between the sun and the moon. So, all of the light reflected from the moon is visible from Earth. The moon, Earth, and sun are aligned with Earth in the middle. The moon's sunlit half, which is its day / (night) side, faces Earth's (day)/ night side. That is always the case on the night of a full moon.

 EVIDENCE NOTEBOOK

17. How does the model of phases of the moon help to explain why we can see the moon in the sky both during the day and at night? Record your evidence.

Engineer It

Plan a Lunar Mission

You are planning an expedition to the moon. Astronauts will stay on the moon for four days to collect samples and data. You want them to land on part of the moon that is lit by the sun so they can see their surroundings. While on the moon, astronauts need to use radio waves to communicate with Earth. For the waves to reach Earth, your radio transmitter must be pointed toward Earth. Because the phases of the moon are predictable, you can choose the best days for the trip years before the launch.

18. During which phase(s) and where on the moon would you want to land? Explain. Draw a diagram to justify your choice.

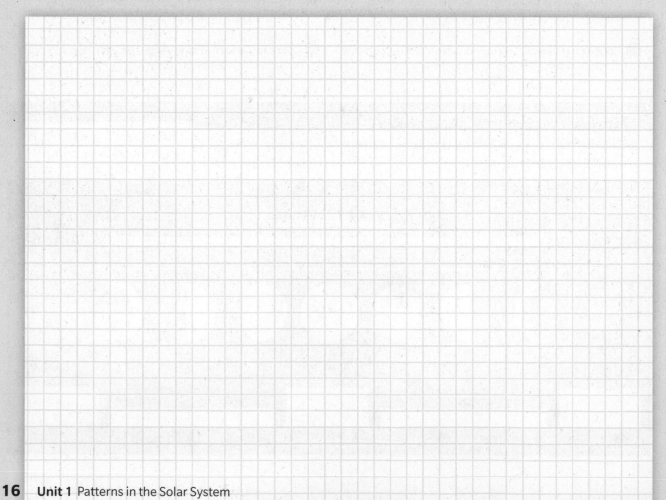

Exploring Eclipses

You can make shadow puppets, such as the one in the photo, using a flashlight and your hands. You can also use paper cutouts to make shadows. Moving the cutout, or your hands, makes the shadow move.

19. In the photo, why does the shadow of a dog's head form on the wall behind the hand?

You can make a shadow puppet of a dog's head using your hand and a light source.

Eclipses

Earth and the moon block the light from the sun and form shadows behind them in space. Sometimes, the moon moves into Earth's shadow or Earth moves into the moon's shadow. Both events are called an *eclipse*. An **eclipse** happens when the shadow of one celestial body falls on another. Both solar and lunar eclipses, shown in the photos below, occur in the Earth-sun-moon system. During a *solar eclipse*, the shadow of the moon falls on Earth. During a *lunar eclipse*, the shadow of Earth falls on the moon.

A solar eclipse: from Earth, we can see the moon come between Earth and the sun.

A lunar eclipse: from Earth, we can see the shadow of Earth falling on the moon.

20. Use what you see in the photos to explain how shadows are formed during a solar eclipse and a lunar eclipse. Include the sun, moon, and Earth in your explanations.

the solar eclipse is when the sun is shining and the moon is right infront of it, it shar
The earth shadow cover some of the moon so that we

Hands-On Lab

Model Solar and Lunar Eclipses

You will model the Earth-sun-moon system to develop an explanation for solar and lunar eclipses.

MATERIALS
- lamp with removable shade
- moon model from previous activity

Procedure and Analysis

STEP 1 Continue working with your partner. The lamp (sun) should be placed at eye level. One partner plays Earth first, completing STEPS 2–4. Then switch roles and have the other partner play Earth. Each partner records their own observations.

STEP 2 **Act** The partner playing Earth faces the sun. Earth holds the moon at arm's length so the moon and the sun are in a straight line with the moon directly between Earth and the sun.

STEP 3 **Act** Earth closes one eye and slowly turns toward the left. As you turn, stop when your view of the moon is completely covered in shadow. Record your observations of the alignment of the Earth-sun-moon system and what you see from Earth.

STEP 4 **Act** Earth continues to turn left. Stop when you notice that the moon blocks your view of the sun. Record your observations.

STEP 5 A solar eclipse happens when the sun is dark, which I observed in the model when _my head / the ball_ was blocking my view of the lamp. A lunar eclipse happens when the moon appears dark. I observed a lunar eclipse when _my head / the lamp_ was putting a shadow on the ball.

STEP 6 If time allows, repeat STEPS 2–4, this time holding the moon slightly above your head. What differences do you see?

In the Shadow of the Moon

Solar eclipses occur when the moon moves between the sun and Earth. The moon blocks some sunlight from reaching Earth. The shadow that extends behind the moon has two cone-shaped parts, modeled in the photo. The darker, inner shadow is the *umbra*. The lighter, larger shadow is the *penumbra*.

At least two solar eclipses occur every year. But, as the diagram below shows, the moon's shadow does not completely cover Earth. Only a small area is covered by the shadow, which is why not everyone on Earth can see every solar eclipse. To see a solar eclipse, you must be in the path of the moon's shadow. The dark umbra covers an even smaller area than the larger penumbra. As an area of Earth passes through the umbra, the sun appears to be totally eclipsed. The sun briefly goes dark, for a few minutes at most. It may seem like nighttime until that area of Earth moves out of the moon's shadow.

The umbra is the darkest part of a shadow. The penumbra is the lighter part of a shadow.

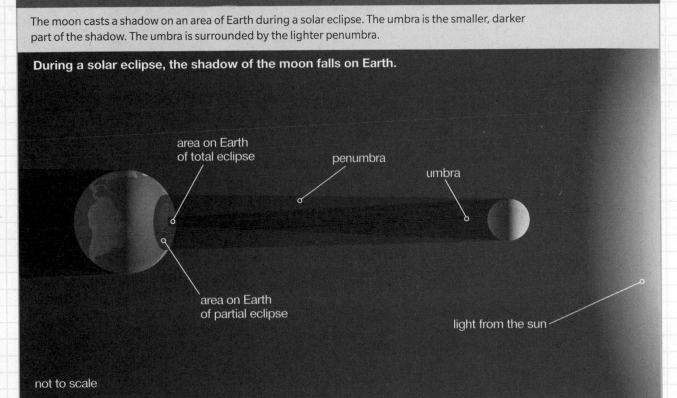

A Solar Eclipse

The moon casts a shadow on an area of Earth during a solar eclipse. The umbra is the smaller, darker part of the shadow. The umbra is surrounded by the lighter penumbra.

During a solar eclipse, the shadow of the moon falls on Earth.

area on Earth of total eclipse

penumbra

umbra

area on Earth of partial eclipse

light from the sun

not to scale

21. During a solar eclipse, the sun appears to go either fully or partially dark. Why can solar eclipses only be observed on certain parts of Earth? Circle all that apply.

A. The moon is smaller than Earth.

B. Only the people in the umbra will see the sun go totally dark.

C. People in the penumbra will see the sun go partially dark.

D. Solar eclipses only occur once every few years.

Types of Solar Eclipses

There are three types of solar eclipses. A *total solar eclipse* occurs when the sun appears to be completely blocked except for a bright halo of light. A total eclipse only happens when the Earth, moon, and sun are in a straight line. An *annular solar eclipse* also occurs when they are in a straight line. However, the moon is farther away from Earth in its orbit, and the umbra shadow does not quite reach Earth. So, the moon does not completely cover the sun. The sun's outer edges can be seen as a ring of light around the darker center during an annular eclipse. When a total eclipse of the sun occurs, only people who observe from the umbra will see the total eclipse. People who observe from the penumbra will see a *partial solar eclipse*, since from their point of view, the moon only blocks part of the sun's light.

Types of Solar Eclipses

22. Write the correct term from the word bank to label each image.

- annular solar eclipse
- ~~uneclipsed sun~~
- partial solar eclipse
- total solar eclipse

uneclipsed sun

Partial Solar eclipse

ahnular

total Solar

In the Shadow of Earth

During a lunar eclipse, Earth is between the moon and the sun. Because Earth is so much bigger than the moon, Earth's shadow covers the entire moon when they are aligned. As the diagram on the following page shows, Earth's shadow also has an umbra and penumbra. Remember, the moon reflects sunlight. When Earth blocks sunlight from reaching the moon, the moon appears dark. Instead of being totally dark, the moon often appears to be a rusty red color because Earth's atmosphere bends some sunlight into the shadow. Everyone who is on the dark side of Earth can see a lunar eclipse because Earth is casting the shadow.

A Lunar Eclipse

During a lunar eclipse, the moon is in Earth's shadow. Little light from the sun reaches the moon.

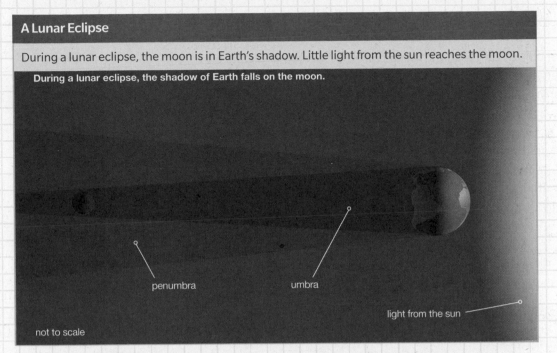

During a lunar eclipse, the shadow of Earth falls on the moon.

penumbra

umbra

light from the sun

not to scale

23. Analyze the image. Then write *all* or *part* to complete the paragraph.

During a lunar eclipse, the moon can become either partially or entirely dark. The outer or *penumbral* shadow is an area where Earth blocks ___all___ of the sun's rays from reaching the moon. In contrast, the inner or *umbral* shadow is a region where Earth blocks ___part___ direct sunlight from reaching the moon.

Types of Lunar Eclipses

During a lunar eclipse, the moon may appear totally or partially dark depending on where it passes through Earth's shadow. The time-lapse photo shows multiple images of the moon taken over about three and a half hours. The photo shows a *total lunar eclipse*, which occurs when the whole moon passes through the umbra. During a *partial lunar eclipse*, only part of the moon passes through the umbra. The part of the moon that passes through Earth's shadow becomes dark. There is one more type of lunar eclipse— the *penumbral lunar eclipse*. It occurs when the moon passes through the penumbra. While total and partial eclipses are easy to observe, penumbral eclipses are difficult to see. The penumbra is a lighter shadow and sunlight still reaches the moon when it passes through this part of Earth's shadow.

As the moon passes through Earth's umbra, more of it becomes dark. It turns a reddish-orange instead of being totally dark because Earth's atmosphere bends sunlight into the shadow.

24. Write *total, partial,* or *penumbral* to complete the paragraph.

If the entire moon passes through the part of Earth's shadow called the umbra, a ___total___ lunar eclipse will occur. If the moon passes only through the penumbra, a ___partial___ lunar eclipse will occur.

Timing of Eclipses

Every time the moon orbits Earth, the moon comes between the sun and Earth, and Earth comes between the moon and the sun. Yet eclipses do not occur every time the moon orbits Earth. To understand why, you need to think of space in three dimensions. Think of the sun and Earth's nearly circular orbit around the sun in a flat plane. The moon's orbit is not in the same plane, although it may appear that way in many two-dimensional diagrams. The moon's orbit is actually tilted about 5° to the Earth-sun plane as the diagram shows. Because of this tilted orbit, the moon is usually above or below Earth during its orbit instead of being aligned in the same plane as Earth. So, the moon and Earth usually do not pass through each other's shadows.

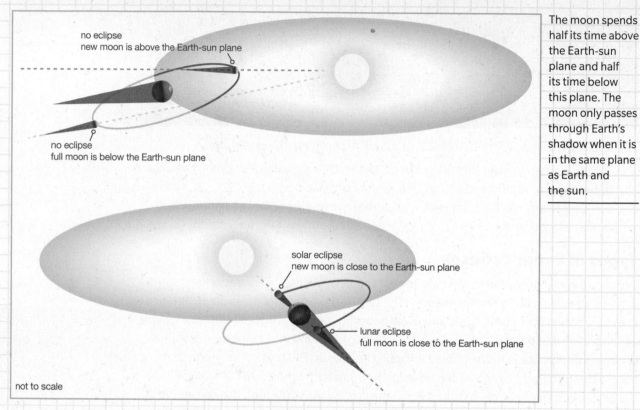

no eclipse
new moon is above the Earth-sun plane

no eclipse
full moon is below the Earth-sun plane

solar eclipse
new moon is close to the Earth-sun plane

lunar eclipse
full moon is close to the Earth-sun plane

not to scale

The moon spends half its time above the Earth-sun plane and half its time below this plane. The moon only passes through Earth's shadow when it is in the same plane as Earth and the sun.

25. Because its orbit is tilted with respect to the Earth-sun plane, the moon spends most of its time either above or below the plane. How many times would the moon cross through the Earth-sun plane each time it orbits Earth? Explain.

Not many because it mostly Passes up or onder Earth

Phases of the Moon During Eclipses

26. What phase will the moon always be in when a solar eclipse happens? When a lunar eclipse happens? Draw diagrams to support your answers.

New Moon

Continue Your Exploration

Name: _____ Date: _____

Check out the path below or go online to choose one of the other paths shown.

People in Science

- **Hands-on Labs** ✋
- **Using Shadows and Shade**
- **Propose Your Own Path**

Go online to choose one of these other paths.

Leon Foucault, Physicist

By 1850, it was widely accepted that Earth rotates on its axis. But a French physicist, Leon Foucault (FOO•koh), was the first person to design an instrument that demonstrated Earth's rotation.

Foucault realized that he could show Earth's rotation using a carefully designed pendulum. A pendulum is a ball that hangs by a wire from a fixed point. Once the ball is released, it swings back and forth. Foucault used a 67-meter-long wire and designed the pendulum so that it could swing in any direction. He hung his first pendulum from the Paris Observatory in 1851. The swinging pendulum appeared to gradually change its direction of swing over the course of a day. This change in direction was evidence that Earth was rotating.

Leon Foucault was a French physicist who designed an experiment to provide evidence that Earth rotates.

Explore ONLINE!

Foucault's pendulum appears to move as Earth rotates under it. Throughout the day, this pendulum knocks down pegs to show how its swing gradually changes direction.

Lesson 1 The Earth-Sun-Moon System **23**

Continue Your Exploration

1. Why was it necessary for Foucault's pendulum to swing freely in all directions in order for it to demonstrate that Earth rotates?

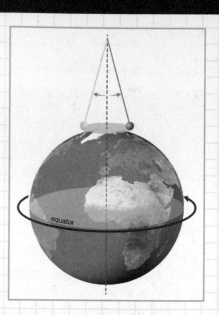

2. How does the explanation for the way Foucault's pendulum appears to move relate to the explanation for why the sun, moon, and stars appear to circle Earth every 24 hours?

 3. Do the Math Locations other than the North and South Poles move in a circle around Earth's axis as Earth rotates. Because of this motion, Foucault's pendulum does not complete a full circle in one day. For example, it only turns 270° in one day in Paris. How many hours would it take to complete one full circle (360°) in Paris?

   A. 11

   B. 18

   C. 27

   D. 32

4. **Collaborate** With a group, prepare a multimedia presentation to explain how Foucault's pendulum works. Consider including videos or demonstrations.

Can You Explain It?

Name: _____   **Date:** _____

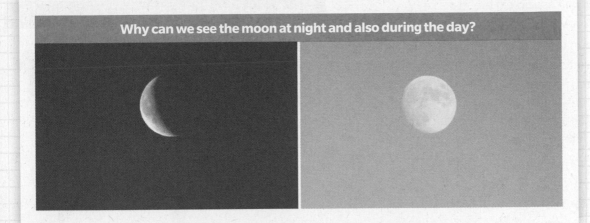

Why can we see the moon at night and also during the day?

EVIDENCE NOTEBOOK

Refer to the notes in your Evidence Notebook to help you construct an explanation for why the moon is visible at night and during the day.

1. State your claim. Make sure your claim fully explains why you can see the moon during the daytime and the nighttime.

2. Summarize the evidence you have gathered to support your claim and explain your reasoning.

Checkpoints

Answer the following questions to check your understanding of the lesson.

Use the map to answer Questions 3-4.

3. The sun will rise first in the Eastern / Pacific Time Zone. As it appears to move across the sky, it will rise in the Central / Mountain Time Zone next. At the end of the day, sunset will occur last in the Eastern / Pacific Time Zone.

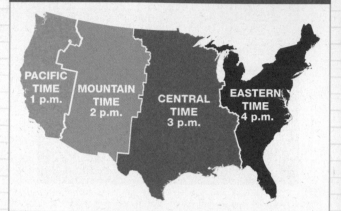

Time Zones in the United States

4. When the sun sets in the Central Time Zone, in which time zones will it be night? Circle all that apply.

   A. Central
   B. Eastern
   C. Mountain
   D. Pacific

Use the photos to answer Questions 5-6.

5. Why are appearances of the moon in each photo different from each other? Circle all that apply.

   A. Both photos show phases of the moon.
   B. The top photo shows an eclipse and the bottom photo shows a phase.
   C. The moon in the bottom photo occurs about once every month.
   D. The moon in the top photo only occurs when the moon is in Earth' shadow.

6. The moon in the bottom photo is in its third quarter. How will the moon look after it moves another quarter of the way through its orbit?

   A. The same as it looks in the photo.
   B. The full circle of the moon will be lit.
   C. The moon will be completely dark.
   D. The quarter moon will be lit on the other side.

7. In August 2017, a total solar eclipse was visible from the United States. A total solar eclipse happens when Earth / the moon moves directly in front of the moon / sun. A total solar eclipse can be seen from everywhere / a narrow path on Earth.

Interactive Review

Complete this section to review the main concepts of the lesson.

The sun, stars, and moon appear to move across the sky because of Earth's rotation.

A. Describe the movement of the sun, stars, and moon across the sky.

The moon goes through a pattern of phases over a period of 29.5 days. Phases change as the fraction of the sunlit area of the moon that is visible from Earth changes.

B. What explains the difference in appearance between a full moon and a new moon? Include the arrangement of the sun, moon, and Earth in your explanation.

Eclipses happen when Earth is in the shadow of the moon or the moon is in the shadow of Earth.

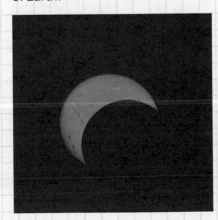

C. Explain the difference between a partial eclipse and a total eclipse. Use either a solar eclipse or a lunar eclipse as an example.

Seasons

Fall leaves change color as weather cools and leaves are no longer able to produce food for the tree. This photo of Virginia's Sherando Lake shows an example of this phenomenon.

By the end of this lesson . . .

you will be able to explain how Earth's shape, tilt, and orbit around the sun cause the seasons of the year.

Go online to view the digital version of the Hands-On Lab for this lesson and to download additional lab resources.

CAN YOU EXPLAIN IT?

Why is winter cold with shorter days than summer?

Explore ONLINE!

A winter day at the Tatra Mountains in Zakopane, Poland.

1. Look at the photo. How do you know this photo was taken in winter?

2. One day is defined as an amount of time equal to 24 hours. Why do you think people say winter days are shorter than summer days?

 EVIDENCE NOTEBOOK As you explore the lesson, gather evidence to help explain why winter days are colder and shorter than summer days are.

Analyzing an Earth-Sun Model to Explain the Stars Seen in the Sky

A group of stars that form a pattern is called a *constellation*. The constellation Ursa Major also has an inner pattern known as the Big Dipper. But if you look for the Big Dipper, you will see that it is not always in the same position in the night sky. In addition to the movement of the stars across the sky every night, their rising times change throughout the year. So the constellations visible in the early evening are different in winter, spring, summer, and fall.

3. Discuss When you look at the night sky, what do you see?

The Big Dipper is one of the most familiar star patterns in the northern sky. It looks like a ladle used to scoop water.

Changes in Stars Seen in the Night Sky

Just as the sun appears to move in a path across the sky, stars in the night sky also appear to move. They seem to change locations nightly.

4. Why do the stars appear to move across the sky every night?

    A. Because Earth orbits the sun once a year.

    B. Because Earth tilts on its axis.

    C. Because Earth rotates once every 24 hours.

5. Act With your class, investigate why star patterns change yearly.

- Several students form a large circle. They represent the stars in the night sky. One student represents the sun and stands in the center. One student represents Earth and stands between the stars and the sun. The head of the student who is Earth represents the North Pole of Earth.

- Earth will move around the sun in a counterclockwise direction. The sun and stars do not move.

- Earth stands facing away from the sun. Earth looks straight ahead, to the left, and to the right. Note which stars Earth can see. This is the night sky in summer.

- Earth moves to a position one-fourth of the way around the sun. Note which stars Earth can see. This is the fall night sky.

- Earth moves to a winter position and finally a spring position. Note how the stars seen in the night sky change.

6. In the activity, if the student playing Earth turns to face the sun, what time of day is it for people who live on that side of Earth? _____
If the person now turns halfway around and looks at the stars, what time of day is it for the same people? _____

7. The student who represents Earth sees different stars from different positions in the circle. How does this model suggest evidence that Earth circles the sun once a year?

Seasonal Star Patterns

Earth's place in its orbit affects which stars can be seen during different seasons. The location of stars in the night sky changes as Earth moves along its orbit. During the year, you will be able to see all the stars visible from one specific place on Earth.

On a given day, you will only be able to see the stars that are in the opposite direction of the sun. The stars seen from the Northern Hemisphere may be different from the stars seen from the Southern Hemisphere. If you are on the North or South Pole, the stars will appear to rotate around a point directly above your head because of Earth's rotation. The sky seen from the North Pole is completely different than the sky seen from the South Pole. As you move from the North Pole toward the South Pole, the sky will change. The sky seen by someone in Florida may have some of the same stars in the sky seen by someone in Brazil, but the whole pattern of stars seen is not the same.

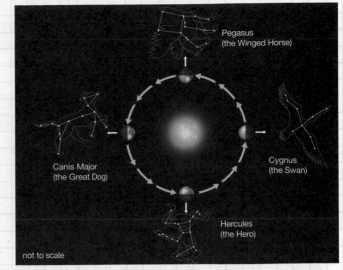

Earth's place in its orbit affects which stars are seen at different times of the year. For example, Cygnus is seen in the night sky of the Northern Hemisphere in summer.

Some Stars Are Seen in Different Seasons

These are some of the constellations visible in the night sky of the Northern Hemisphere during **winter**. During the day, the sun blocks summer constellations from sight.

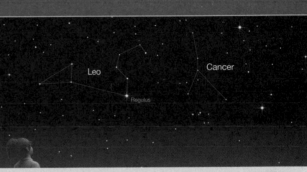

As Earth continues its orbit around the sun, winter changes to **spring**. Earth faces a different direction during the night and new constellations become visible.

In **fall**, Earth is three-fourths of the way through its orbit around the sun and new constellations are visible. Soon, winter constellations will start to be seen once more.

Earth's **summer** position brings new constellations into view. Now the winter constellations are opposite the sun and cannot be seen.

8. Why do you see different stars in spring's night sky than in fall's night sky? Explain.

These photos, taken at about the same time of night, show the position of the Big Dipper from season to season in the Northern Hemisphere.

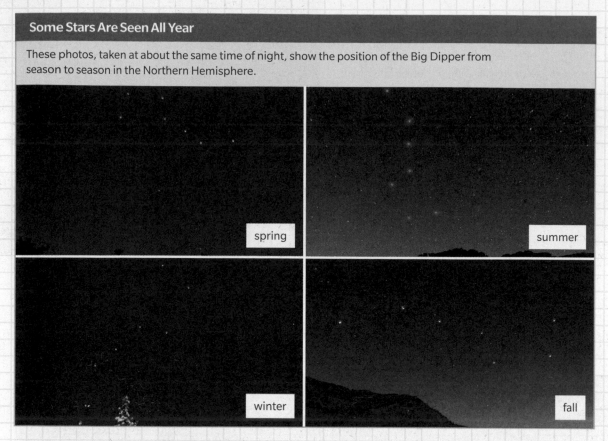

spring

summer

winter

fall

Earth's place in its orbit determines which stars can be seen during different seasons, but depending on how far north or south of the equator you are, there are some stars that can be seen in the sky all year. Your location on Earth determines which stars stay visible all year.

9. Circle the correct words to explain what you observe in the photos above.

The Big Dipper appears to *keep / change* its position from season to season.
The Big Dipper seems to move in a circular pattern as the *seasons / years* change.

Navigation Using the Stars

In the Northern Hemisphere, the North Star's position remains fixed in place throughout the year because Earth's north axis points to it.

Because it does not shift position, the North Star became a guide by which sailors could navigate the northern seas at night. At the North Pole, the North Star is seen directly overhead. At the equator, the North Star is seen at the horizon. By taking a measure of the angle of elevation of the North Star, you can determine your latitude on Earth.

10. Could a person at the South Pole see the North Star? Explain.

_____

_____

_____

_____

Time-lapse photography was used to capture this image over the course of one night. The sky is photographed at regular intervals to show the slow, continuous movement of other stars around the North Star.

Relating Seasons to Energy from the Sun

During a year, many places on Earth experience four seasons. *Winter* is generally cold and may bring snow and ice. As temperatures warm, snow melts and *spring* begins. Next comes *summer*, the warmest season. *Fall* (also called *autumn*) follows, temperatures get cooler, and then winter begins again.

11. What seasonal changes do you see where you live?

Snow
wind   *Rain*
Sunlite

Early blooms announce that spring is on the way and winter is ending.

Seasons of the Year

A **season** is a division of the year that is associated with particular weather patterns and daylight hours. Weather conditions and daily temperatures at any location on Earth follow a predictable cycle throughout the year. Winter may be cold. Summer may be hot. Spring and fall temperatures are warmer than winter's but colder than summer's. The farther north you go, the greater the differences in the seasons. For example, areas closer to the equator have milder weather in winter than areas closer to the poles have.

The Four Seasons of the Year

spring

In the Northern Hemisphere, spring begins In March. The sun moves higher across the sky and the number of daylight hours increases. Temperatures gradually rise.

summer

Summer is the warmest season, beginning in June in the Northern Hemisphere. The sun is in the sky for a greater part of the day.

winter

In December, the Northern Hemisphere begins its coldest season—winter. Freezing temperatures and snowfall are associated with winter months. The sun sets early in the day.

fall

Fall begins in September in the Northern Hemisphere. The number of daylight hours decreases as the sun's path across the sky moves lower. Temperatures gradually cool.

Changes across the Seasons

Because of Earth's rotation, we see the sun appear to move across the sky. For people living on the equator, the path of the sun in the sky does not change very much throughout the year. The sun rises on the eastern horizon, goes nearly overhead, and then sets on the western horizon. The sun reaches its highest point in the sky at about noon. Daytime lasts about 12 hours all year long, and the weather is nearly always warm. But as you move north or south away from the equator, the sun's path in the sky changes during the year. For example, in the Northern Hemisphere, the sun rises north of east in the summer. In winter, the sun rises south of east. Sunsets follow the same pattern. Summer sunsets in the Northern Hemisphere are north of west, while winter sunsets are south of west. The sun's path changes as seasons change.

The Path of the Sun in Summer and Winter in the Northern Hemisphere

12. Write summer or winter to label each path of the sun.

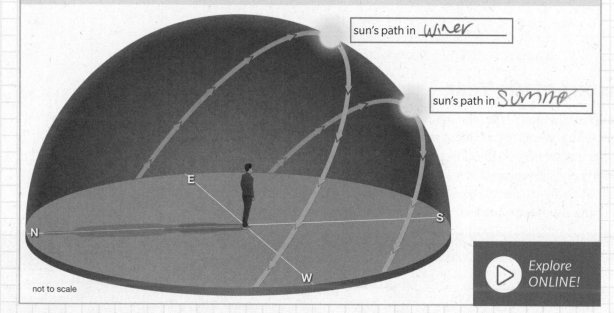

sun's path in _Winter_

sun's path in _Summer_

not to scale

Explore ONLINE!

Daylight Hours

In winter, it may be dark when you wake up for school and dark again soon after school ends. The sun does not go very high in the sky so its path across the sky is shorter. Because the sun is not up in the sky very long, there is less daylight time during this time of year. There is less time for the sunlight to heat up Earth during the daytime and more time for Earth to cool during the longer nighttime hours. The shortest amount of daylight time is on December 21 or 22 in the Northern Hemisphere.

In summer, the sun goes higher in the sky. Days are longer because it takes more time for the sun to complete its longer path across the sky. It is warmer in summer than in winter because the sun is up for a longer period of time. There are more hours of daylight to warm Earth during daytime, and fewer nighttime hours for Earth to cool. The day with the greatest amount of daylight time is June 20, 21, or 22 in the Northern Hemisphere.

13. How is the number of daylight hours of sunlight related to the seasons?

When it is summer it's not.

day light

Hands-On Lab
Model Sunlight Distribution

 Do the Math You will explore what happens when light is spread out compared to when it is not spread out.

MATERIALS
- flashlight
- graph paper
- metric ruler
- pencil
- protractor

Procedure

STEP 1 Work with a partner. One partner shines a flashlight straight down on graph paper from a height of 15 cm. Using a protractor, the second partner makes sure the light strikes the paper at a 90° angle. The second partner then traces around the lit area on the paper with a pencil. Label it *90°*.

STEP 2 Switch holding the flashlight between partners. Keep the flashlight at the same height as it was in STEP 1 (15 cm). Using the protractor, one partner guides the other to change the position of the flashlight so that the angle of the light striking the paper is 60°. That partner traces the lit area and labels it *60°*.

STEP 3 Next, using the protractor, change the angle so that the light striking the paper is 30°. Trace the lit area and label it *30°*.

STEP 4 Calculate the total area of each lit area using this method:

  a. Count and record the number of full squares in each area.
  Example: 4 full squares

  b. Count the number of partial squares and divide the number by 2.
  Example: 12 partial squares ÷ 2 = 6

  c. Add the number of full squares to the number calculated for partial squares to find the total area. Example: 4 + 6 = 10

Angle of light	4a. Full squares	4b. Partial squares	4c. Total area
90°			
60°			
30°			

Analysis

STEP 5 Compare the total areas. What do you think the data mean?

Energy from the Sun

There are two reasons why we receive different amounts of the sun's energy in summer and winter: changes in the length of the sun's path across the sky and changes in the height of the sun in the middle of the day. In the summer, the sun has a longer path across the sky, which means the sun is in the sky for a longer period of time. There are more hours of daylight, so there is more time for Earth to absorb the solar energy.

The height of the sun in the sky determines the angle at which the sunlight strikes Earth. As shown in the activity, when the sun is overhead, the energy on each square meter is more intense—the light is less spread out. The amount of energy striking a smaller area will result in warmer temperatures than the same amount of energy striking a spread-out area. In summer, when the sun is higher in the sky, the solar energy is more intense. In winter, when the sun is lower in the sky, the sun's energy reaches Earth at a lesser angle. Solar energy passes through more atmosphere when it strikes Earth at a lesser angle, making the sun's rays striking Earth less intense. The angle at which sunlight strikes Earth influences Earth's temperatures, making it hot in summer and cold in winter. These changes in the sun's path across the sky and the angle at which sunlight strikes Earth affect the changes in temperature that occur across the seasons.

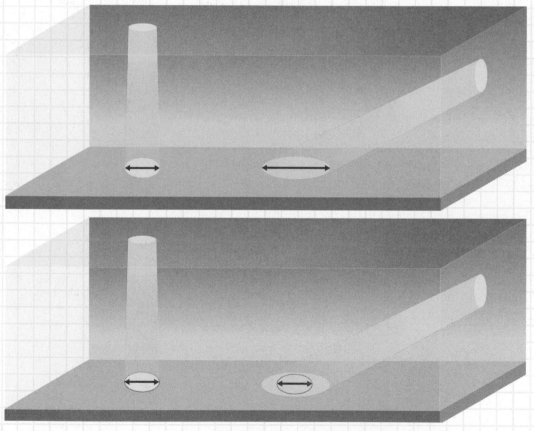

As the sun moves lower in the sky, the energy from sunlight is spread over a larger and larger area. The same amount of ground gets all of the light when the sun is directly overhead, but gets only a part of the light when the sun strikes at an angle.

14. **Discuss** Together with a partner, talk about the amount of solar energy that falls on a given area. What happens when light is not spread out? What happens when the light is more spread out? Relate this idea to the sun's energy and Earth.

When it is more spread out it is less intense

15. Language SmArts On a separate sheet of paper, write a short essay to compare what you observed in your investigation to what you saw in the image and what you read about the angles of sunlight striking Earth.

EVIDENCE NOTEBOOK

16. How do the length of days and the path of the sun across the sky help to explain why winter is cold with shorter days? Record your evidence.

Patterns of Sunlight and Latitude

Light comes from the sun. The rays of sunlight move in straight lines. Because the sun is so far away, the rays that strike Earth are very nearly parallel. Because of Earth's spherical shape, these parallel rays strike Earth most directly at the equator. As you move from the equator to the poles, the rays strike at lesser angles.

The diagram shows Earth lit by the sun on a day in the spring or fall. The diagram shows that the sun appears overhead as viewed from the equator. So, people who live on or near the equator feel the intense energy of the sun. People who live at the North Pole would see the sun on this same day as very low in the sky. This helps to illustrate why it is nearly always warm near the equator and cold at the poles.

polar region

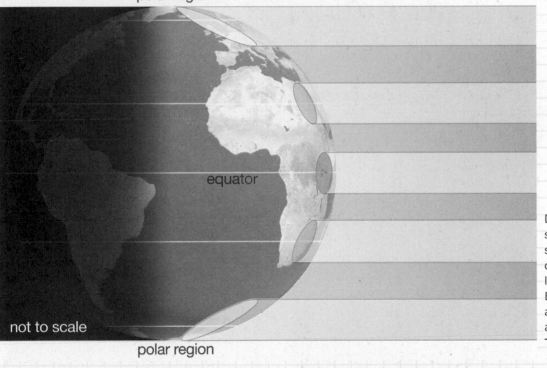

equator

not to scale

polar region

Due to the shape of Earth, sunlight strikes different latitudes on Earth's surface at different angles.

17. Think about a person at the equator, a person at the North Pole, and a person somewhere in between. Each person points toward the sun. Describe where in the sky they are pointing.

The sun is in the east

18. Which of these describes the differences in sunlight striking Earth at different latitudes? Circle all that apply.

   A. The intensity of the sun's energy received at the equator is greater than the intensity of the energy received at the poles.

   B. Sunlight strikes at a greater angle at the equator, which spreads out the sunlight.

   C. As you move away from the equator, the rays of sunlight striking Earth are no longer parallel.

   D. Sunlight passes through less atmosphere at the equator, so more sunlight gets through, which makes locations around the equator hotter.

Analyze How Earth's Shape Affects Patterns of Sunlight

19. If Earth were flat instead of curved, how would that affect temperatures from pole to pole? Explain how the range of temperatures at noon at different latitudes on a cube-shaped planet would compare to temperatures on our spherical Earth.

   The Poles would recived more
   Sun light sitec to Sun rays meall
   in Parrale ióg

20. **Draw** To the right of the cube, draw a model of the way the sun's rays would strike a cube-shaped planet.

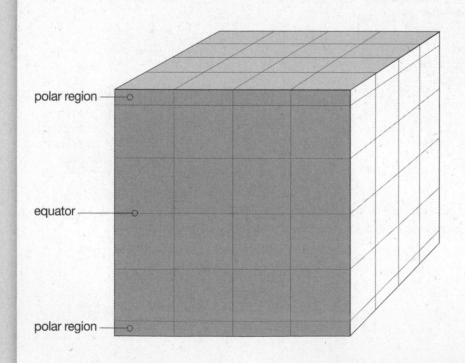

polar region

equator

polar region

Analyzing an Earth-Sun Model to Explain Seasons

Earth orbits the sun in a predictable pattern. The pattern of Earth's seasons depends on how much sunlight reaches different areas of Earth as the planet moves around the sun. One complete orbit around the sun is called a *revolution*. One complete revolution takes one year.

Earth-Sun Models

Earth has a nearly circular orbit around the sun. Earth also rotates around its north-south axis, an imaginary line passing through Earth from pole to pole.

21. Examine the image. What does this model show? Circle all that apply.

    A. Every place on the planet gets 12 hours of light and 12 hours of dark each day.

    B. Temperature conditions on the planet change depending on distance from the sun.

    C. There are colder temperatures at the poles and warmer temperatures at the equator, but no temperature changes during the year.

22. Does this first model explain the seasons that happen on Earth? Give at least one example to support your answer.

    The tilt is explained in different Positions

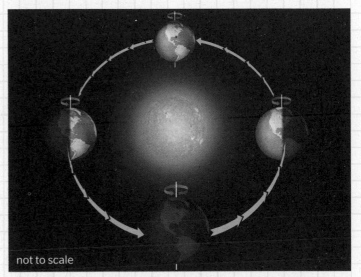

not to scale

Earth has a nearly circular orbit around the sun. This model of a fictional Earth shows an axis that is not tilted.

Unlike the planet in the first model, Earth's axis is not perpendicular to the plane of Earth's orbit around the sun. Earth's axis is tilted 23.5° from perpendicular to the plane of its orbit. This tilt remains the same throughout Earth's orbit. Earth's axis is pointed in the same direction no matter where Earth is in its orbit around the sun.

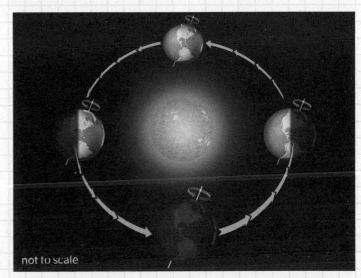

not to scale

This model shows Earth with its axis tilted 23.5°.

Hands-On Lab
Model Patterns of Sunlight throughout Earth's Revolution

You will model the tilt of Earth. You will show the way different areas of Earth receive more or less sunlight throughout the year.

MATERIALS
- construction paper
- foam ball, 1"
- light source
- marker
- metric ruler
- modeling clay, non-drying
- protractor
- toothpick

Procedure

STEP 1 Use clay to make a base for your foam ball sphere.

STEP 2 With the marker, mark both poles and draw an equator on the sphere. Push the toothpick carefully through the sphere from pole to pole.

STEP 3 Insert the toothpick into the base. Using the protractor, set the tilt of the axis at 23.5° from vertical.

STEP 4 Cut the construction paper so that it is a square and then fold it exactly in half. Draw a line along the fold. Use the protractor to mark 90° on both sides of the line and connect those marks. Label the four connected folds beginning with *Spring* and moving counterclockwise to label *Summer*, *Fall*, and *Winter*.

STEP 5 Place the light source on the center where the lines cross. This is your sun.

STEP 6 Set the sphere directly on *Summer*. The North Pole (top of the toothpick) should tilt toward the light. Observe where the sphere is light and dark. Record your data by drawing and shading to show your *Summer* sphere in the table below.

STEP 7 **Keep the angle and direction that the sphere is pointing the same.** Move the sphere to *Fall*. Observe where the light falls. Record your data in the table for *Fall*.

STEP 8 Repeat STEP 7, moving the sphere to *Winter* and then *Spring*.

Summer	Fall	Winter	Spring

Analysis

STEP 9 What did you observe about sunlight on Earth in winter? Why does the Northern Hemisphere have lower temperatures in winter? Use what you observed to explain.

STEP 10 Look at the sphere. When the Northern Hemisphere tilts away from the sun, what season would you expect to experience in the Southern Hemisphere? Why?

The Tilt of Earth

The spherical shape of Earth explains why it gets colder as you get closer to the poles, and why the height of the sun appears lower in the sky as you get closer to the poles. But these ideas alone do not completely explain why it is warmer in summer than in winter.

What did you learn as your model Earth moved around the model sun? Because Earth's tilt did not change, the amount of sunlight reaching a specific area of Earth did change. As Earth orbits the sun, the area of Earth that is pointed more toward the sun changes because Earth is always tilted in the same direction. So, the reason we have seasons is because of a combination of Earth's tilt and Earth's revolution.

When the Northern Hemisphere points toward the sun, the Southern Hemisphere points away from the sun. Seasons in the Southern Hemisphere are opposite from those in the Northern Hemisphere. In December, it is winter in Canada and summer in Australia.

23. Do the North and South Poles always stay in the same position relative to the sun? Explain your reasoning.

It is Earth is at at slight tilt so the Poles are at the bottom and don't really move

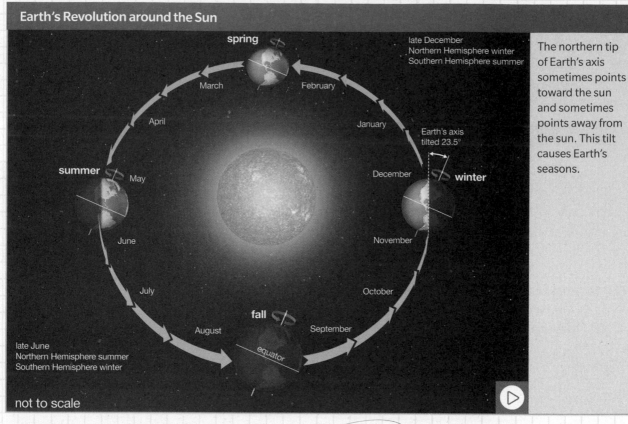

Earth's Revolution around the Sun

spring

late December
Northern Hemisphere winter
Southern Hemisphere summer

March

February

April

January

Earth's axis
tilted 23.5°

summer

May

December

winter

June

November

July

October

fall

August

September

equator

late June
Northern Hemisphere summer
Southern Hemisphere winter

not to scale

The northern tip of Earth's axis sometimes points toward the sun and sometimes points away from the sun. This tilt causes Earth's seasons.

24. It is summer in the hemisphere tilted ~~away from~~ / toward ⃝ the sun. It is winter in the hemisphere tilted ⃝away from⃝ / ~~toward~~ the sun. The seasons are ~~the same~~ / ⃝reversed⃝ in the Northern and Southern Hemispheres.

The Effect of Earth's Tilt on Daylight Hours

The number of hours of daylight increases as spring changes to summer. This change is the result of Earth's tilt. If Earth had no tilt, days and nights would last about 12 hours each day everywhere. Because of the tilt, areas pointed toward the sun have more hours of daylight than those areas pointed away.

Hours of Daylight by Latitude

25. Complete the labels to show how much daylight an area at each latitude would have with Earth in this position.

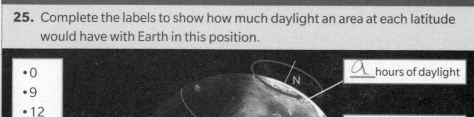

- 0
- 9
- 12
- ~~15~~
- 24

N

_a_ hours of daylight

_15_ hours of daylight

_24_ hours of daylight

_12_ hours of daylight

_0_ hours of daylight

not to scale

S

The Solstices and Equinoxes

Solstices mark the two days of the year when Earth's axis is tilted directly toward or away from the sun. The June solstice, also called the summer solstice, occurs when Earth's north axis is tilted toward the sun, between June 20 and June 22. The June solstice is the day of the year with the greatest number of daylight hours in the Northern Hemisphere. This longest day of the year in the Northern Hemisphere is at the same time as the shortest day of the year in the Southern Hemisphere.

The December solstice, also called the winter solstice, occurs when Earth's north axis is tilted away from the sun, around December 21. The December solstice is the day with the fewest number of daylight hours in the Northern Hemisphere. In the Southern Hemisphere, the December solstice is the longest day of the year.

The days that begin spring and fall are marked by the equinoxes. Earth's axis does not tilt directly toward or away from the sun. The word *equinox* means "equal night." On an equinox, there are equal hours of day and night at all locations on Earth.

On the June solstice, there are 24 hours of daylight at the North Pole, 12 hours of daylight at the equator, and 24 hours of darkness at the South Pole.

26. The ~~solstices~~ / equinoxes mark the dates on which Earth's axis is tilted directly toward or away from the sun. The days get shorter / longer as you move from the June solstice to the December solstice in the Northern Hemisphere.

The Tilt of Earth Affects the Energy Received from the Sun

Earth's tilt affects the temperatures at different locations on Earth. Because of Earth's tilt, some parts of Earth receive more solar energy than others. At the North Pole, Earth's tilt means that the sun rises above the horizon in mid-March and continues to shine until mid-September. The sun does not completely set during that time. But since the sun shines on the North Pole at a lesser angle instead of striking from directly overhead, less energy is received in a given area at the North Pole than at the equator. When sunlight strikes at a lesser angle, the light spreads out. So, although daylight lasts longer at the North Pole than at the equator, the temperature is not as warm.

The angle at which sunlight strikes a particular location on Earth changes as Earth revolves around the sun. Areas are warmer when sunlight is not as spread out, such as in those areas around the equator.

27. When the South Pole is tilted toward / ~~away from~~ the sun, the Southern Hemisphere experiences winter. The amount of the sun's energy that strikes the area increases / decreases as compared to the sun's energy in the summer. The daylight hours are longer / shorter, and the area temperatures increase / decrease.

So, Earth's distance from the sun is not what determines the seasons. In fact, Earth is closest to the sun around January 3 and farthest from the sun around July 4. It is Earth's tilt that determines the seasons.

28. How can the tilt of Earth be used in an explanation of why winter has cold temperatures and short daylight hours? Record your evidence.

Relate Patterns of Sunlight and Solar Panels

Solar panels capture light from the sun and convert the solar energy to electrical energy. The more sunlight that reaches your solar panels, the more electrical energy you can generate.

How would you position solar panels to receive the maximum amount of light energy from the sun? You know that when the sun's energy is less spread out, the amount of energy reaching that location on Earth is greatest. One way to get maximum light energy to the solar panels is by changing the angle of the panels to directly face the sun. The best angle at which the panels catch the sun depends on how close to the equator the panels are located.

29. Engineer It An engineer must decide how to set up a field of solar panels. Which of these should the engineer consider in order to capture the maximum amount of light energy? Circle all that apply.

A. how far away the location of the solar panel field is from the equator

B. that the panels will be closer to the sun in the summer than in the winter

C. whether the solar panels can be adjusted to a 90° angle to face the incoming light rays

D. whether the panels should face north, south, east, or west

These solar panels are adjusted to the best angle at which to capture solar energy.

30. Look at the solar panels shown in the photo. The photo was taken at noon. Do you think these panels are in an area close or far from the equator? Explain.

_____

_____

_____

_____

_____

Continue Your Exploration

Name: _____   Date: _____

Check out the path below or go online to choose one of the other paths shown.

Land of the Midnight Sun

- **Hands-On Labs** ✋
- **Exploring Ways Organisms Adjust to the Seasons**
- **Propose Your Own Path**

Go online to choose one of these other paths.

The *land of the midnight sun* describes parts of Earth where, for at least some of the year, a part of the sun is visible above the horizon for 24 hours of the day, including at midnight. Midnight sun occurs in the summer months in places north of the Arctic Circle and south of the Antarctic Circle.

Day and night at the poles are not at all like day and night on the rest of Earth. At the poles, there are six months of daylight and then six months of darkness in a year. So, the poles experience one sunrise and one sunset each year.

Areas inside the Arctic and Antarctic Circles also experience periods during the year in which there is darkness or daylight for more than 24 hours. But as you move farther away from the poles these periods get shorter. Locations between the Arctic Circle and the equator and between the Antarctic Circle and the equator do not have days with a midnight sun.

During summer in the Arctic, the sun travels in a complete circle near the horizon but does not set. This time-lapse photo was taken at ten-minute intervals before and after midnight.

1. If the sun is out all day, why is it not warm during an Arctic summer?

Continue Your Exploration

2. When people above the Arctic Circle are experiencing the midnight sun, what are people at the South Pole experiencing?

   A. long nights with only a few hours of sunlight

   B. equal hours of day and night

   C. stars and 24-hour nights

   D. 24-hour nights and a clear view of the North Star

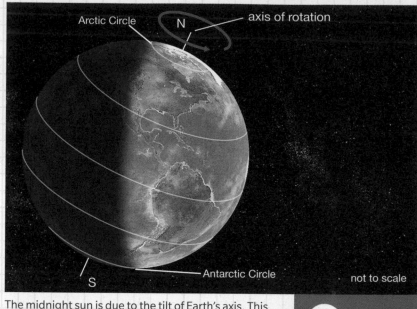

Explore ONLINE!

The midnight sun is due to the tilt of Earth's axis. This image shows Earth's orientation to the sun during summer in the Northern Hemisphere.

3. **Draw** Sketch a model of Earth similar to the one above, but instead show Earth when the areas near the South Pole are experiencing midnight sun. Indicate where sunlight falls and where it is dark. Label Earth's axis and indicate the area south of the Antarctic Circle.

4. **Collaborate** Work with a partner to create a poster that explains the midnight sun. Include some kind of labeled diagram on your poster.

Can You Explain It?

Name: _____ Date: _____

Why is winter cold with shorter days than summer?

 EVIDENCE NOTEBOOK

Refer to the notes in your Evidence Notebook to help you construct an explanation for why winter is cold with shorter days than summer.

1. State your claim. Make sure your claim fully explains the temperature and daylight differences between winter and summer.

2. Summarize the evidence you have gathered to support your claim and explain your reasoning.

Checkpoints

Answer the following questions to check your understanding of the lesson.

Use the photo to answer Question 3.

3. Which of these statements is shown by the photo?

    A. The Southern Hemisphere is in summer and the Northern Hemisphere is in winter.

    B. Both polar regions are experiencing day and nighttime hours of relatively equal length.

    C. The Southern Hemisphere is closer to the sun than the Northern Hemisphere.

Use the diagram to answer Questions 4 and 5.

4. How would the seasons on Uranus compare to the seasons of Earth?

    A. The four seasons of Uranus would be different from Earth's because the tilt of Uranus is different.

    B. Seasons on Uranus would be exactly opposite of seasons on Earth.

    C. Uranus rotates on its side, so Uranus would not experience different seasons.

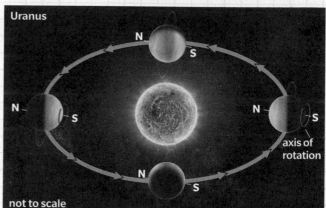

5. Which of these describes the seasons on Uranus?

    A. Uranus has two seasons, summer and winter.

    B. Summer and winter each last for about half of Uranus's complete orbit, with very short spring and fall seasons.

    C. When it is summer in the Northern Hemisphere of Uranus, the Southern Hemisphere has no daylight hours.

6. Which of these are affected by Earth's tilt? Circle all that apply.

    A. the number of daylight hours in June

    B. changes in yearly temperatures across the seasons

    C. how long each season lasts

7. Which statement about stars in the night sky is true?

    A. People in Alaska and in Florida are likely to see the same stars over the course of a night, but the stars may be in a different location in the sky.

    B. When viewed from the same location at the same time of night, stars visible in December may or may not be seen in March.

    C. Stars seen from the Northern Hemisphere in the fall are only seen from the Southern Hemisphere in the spring.

Interactive Review

Complete this section to review the main concepts of the lesson.

We see different parts of the night sky at different times of the year because of Earth's revolution around the sun.

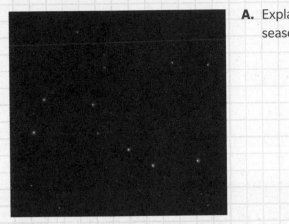

A. Explain why different stars are seen in the sky in different seasons. Discuss both Earth and the sun in your explanation.

The path of the sun across the sky and energy from the sun can help to explain the seasons of the year.

B. How does the path of the sun affect the energy received by Earth at any particular location on Earth?

Earth's tilt and position in its revolution determine the amount of the sun's energy that strikes any particular location on Earth.

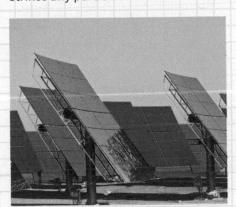

C. Explain why Earth's tilt is responsible for the seasons.

Lesson 2 Seasons **49**

Choose one of the activities to explore how this unit connects to other topics.

☐ Social Studies Connection

Mythological Explanations of the Seasons

Throughout history many different cultures have created stories and explanations to make sense of the changing of the seasons. The ancient Greeks and Native Americans both used stories, called myths, to explain the changing seasons.

Research one Ancient Greek myth and one Native American myth that explain the seasons. Compare and contrast the two myths. Create a presentation with images showing the similarities and differences between the ways these cultures viewed the changes in seasons.

☐ Life Science Connection

Growing Seasons in Different Regions A growing season is the period of the year when crops and other plants grow successfully. The length of a growing season varies with location. On average, most crops need a growing season of at least 90 days.

Research the growing seasons for Alaska and one other state. Organize the data in a multimedia presentation to compare and contrast the lengths of the growing seasons, types of plants that can be grown, and the latitudes of both states. Explain how these factors relate to the ways seasons may differ in the two locations.

☐ Math Connection

Leap Year Archaeological discoveries, such as this ancient Egyptian calendar carved on a stone wall, show that, even thousands of years ago, various cultures tracked time by using calendars.

A leap year is a year that contains one extra calendar day on February 29th. In the Gregorian calendar, most years that are multiples of four are leap years. Research the history behind leap years and determine why we add a day to our calendar every four years. Find out when and how the need for a leap year was first calculated and why the leap year system works. Write a short essay of your findings about leap years and present it to the class.

Name: _____   Date: _____

Complete this review to check your understanding of the unit.

Use the data table to answer Questions 1 and 2.

1. Earth is closest to the sun in *March / June / September / December.*
   It is farthest from the sun in *March / June / September / December.*

Earth's Distance from the Sun in Different Months	
Month	Average Distance of Earth from the Sun (km)
March	149,000,000
June	153,000,000
September	150,000,000
December	148,000,000

2. The data in the table provides evidence that, for the Northern Hemisphere, Earth is closer to the sun in *summer / winter* than it is in the *summer / winter.*

Use the image to answer Questions 3–5.

3. During a *new moon / full moon*, the moon is between Earth and the sun. During a *new moon / full moon*, the moon and sun are on opposite sides of Earth.

4. What is true about when the moon can be seen from any single location on Earth? Select all that apply.

   A. The new moon is in the sky mostly during daylight hours, but is not visible from Earth.

   B. The moon is visible from any location on Earth at all times, day and night, but appears in different phases during each month.

   C. The full moon is seen mostly during nighttime hours.

An Earth-Sun-Moon Model

5. A solar eclipse could happen when the moon is in *position A / position B.*

6. Complete the table by explaining how each component of the Earth-sun-moon system is related to each big concept.

Component	Relative positions and movements	Cause and effect	Patterns
Earth	Earth completes one revolution around the sun every 365.25 days (1 year). Earth completes one rotation every 24 hours. Earth's axis is tilted at a 23.5° angle.		
sun			
moon			

Name: _____   Date: _____

Use the images to answer Questions 7–10.

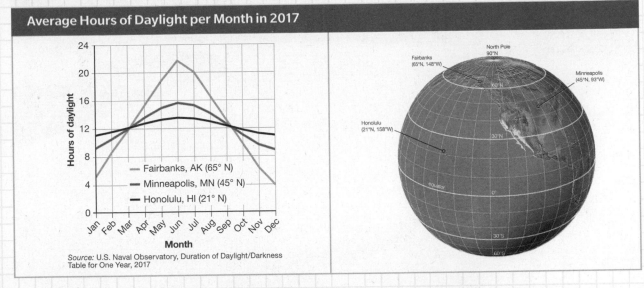

Average Hours of Daylight per Month in 2017

Source: U.S. Naval Observatory, Duration of Daylight/Darkness Table for One Year, 2017

7. Describe the location of each of these cities relative to the equator: Honolulu, Minneapolis, and Fairbanks.

8. What relationship can you identify between latitude of a location and the pattern of daylight hours throughout the year?

9. What can you infer about the difference of seasonal temperature changes in Honolulu, Minneapolis, and Fairbanks? Explain your reasoning.

10. Based on these patterns, what could you infer about the pattern of daylight hours over a year and the seasonal temperature changes for a location on the equator?

Analyze the shadow patterns in the photo to answer Questions 11–15.

11. What causes shadows?

12. Why do the length and direction of a shadow change throughout the day?

13. How are shadows related to lunar phases? to eclipses?

14. How are shadows related to seasons?

15. How do the relative positions of Earth, the sun, and the moon cause shadows to appear differently at different times of the day and year?

Name: _____   Date: _____

How can you model the Earth-sun-moon system?

The third-grade class at your school is studying the solar system. The students are having trouble visualizing and understanding how Earth, the moon, and the sun are part of a system. They specifically struggle with the ideas involving moon phases, eclipses, and seasons. Develop a working model to explain how Earth, the moon, and the sun are related and cause these natural phenomena.

not to scale

The steps below will help guide you in developing and using a working model of the Earth-sun-moon system.

Engineer It

1. **Define the Problem** What are the components you need to include in your system? Components can be matter or energy.

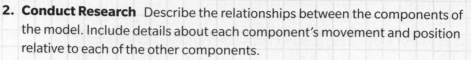

Engineer It

2. **Conduct Research** Describe the relationships between the components of the model. Include details about each component's movement and position relative to each of the other components.

3. **Design a Model** Discuss with your group and determine what criteria and constraints you will use to create a working model of the Earth-sun-moon system. A model could be a drawing, sketch, diagram, animation, diorama, 3-D object, or any other creative way to display the information. Create a rough draft of your design that includes sketches and labels.

4. **Develop a Model** Using the materials you have chosen, construct the Earth-sun-moon system model.

5. **Communicate** Present your model to a 3rd grade class. Use the model to demonstrate moon phases, eclipses, and seasons. Be prepared to answer questions about how the model was built and its limitations.

✓ **Self-Check**

	I identified all of the components of the system and described their movements and positions relative to one another.
	I identified the criteria and constraints for the model and designed and constructed a model that represents the Earth-sun-moon system.
	I used the model to demonstrate the relationships between Earth, the sun, and the moon that result in lunar phases, eclipses, and seasons on Earth.
	I described how the model was built and its limitations.

The Solar System and Universe

From Earth, we can see numerous stars and galaxies. The bright band of stars in this image is the Milky Way galaxy, which is home to Earth and our solar system.

Humans have always been drawn to space. Imagine looking into the night sky and not having an explanation for the hundreds of stars you see. Although we have answered many questions about space, those same questions have led us to more questions that are yet to be answered. In this unit, you will explore Earth's place in the solar system and in the universe. You will analyze the structure and formation of different objects in the solar system. You will discover how objects in space are related.

Why It Matters

Here are some questions to consider as you work through the unit. Can you answer any of the questions now? Revisit these questions at the end of the unit to apply what you discover.

Questions	Notes
How is Earth similar to and different from other objects in space?	
What evidence do scientists use to study and understand the universe?	
What makes up the universe?	
How did the solar system form?	
How can the universe be described as a system?	
What role does gravity play in Earth's place in the universe?	

Unit Starter: Interpret Scale on a Map

The map shows a circular shadow of the moon on Earth during a solar eclipse in 2017 and the path the shadow took as it moved across Earth. Use the map's scale to measure the size of the shadow.

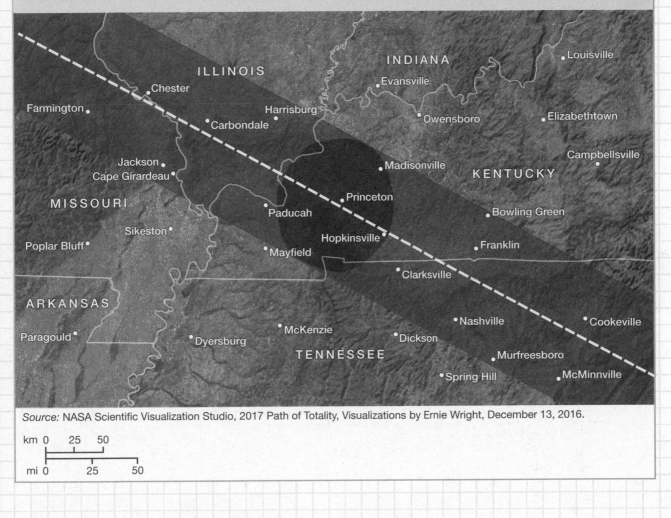

Source: NASA Scientific Visualization Studio, 2017 Path of Totality, Visualizations by Ernie Wright, December 13, 2016.

km 0   25   50

mi 0   25   50

1. Which statement describes the size of the moon's shadow on Earth's surface?

   A. It is equal to the actual size of the moon.

   B. It is larger than the actual size of the moon.

   C. It is smaller than the actual size of the moon.

   D. It is equal to the size of Earth's shadow during a lunar eclipse.

Go online to download the Unit Project Worksheet to help you plan your project.

Unit Project

Museum Model

Build a model of the Milky Way galaxy for a museum or community park. Use the engineering design process to develop a proposal for your installation. Use the model to describe the scale of objects in the universe.

The Formation of the Solar System

Scientists use technology to understand the events that formed the solar system billions of years ago.

By the end of this lesson . . .

you will be able to provide evidence for how the solar system formed.

Go online to view the digital version of the Hands-On Lab for this lesson and to download additional lab resources.

CAN YOU EXPLAIN IT?

Why do all the planets in the solar system orbit the sun in the same direction?

Planets are always in motion. The planets in the solar system follow paths—or *orbits*—around the sun. Each planet also rotates on an axis. While this image shows all planets orbiting the sun, the distances and the planets are not drawn to scale.

 *Explore* ONLINE!

1. How does the sun influence the movement of the planets?

2. Do you think the fact that all planets in the solar system orbit the sun in the same direction is evidence for how our solar system formed? Explain your answer.

 EVIDENCE NOTEBOOK As you explore the lesson, gather evidence to explain why all planets in the solar system orbit the sun in the same direction.

Exploring the Structure of the Solar System

The solar system formed around 4.5 billion years ago. The solar system includes Earth and the planets, dwarf planets, asteroids, comets, and other objects that orbit the sun. The sun is not the only star that has orbiting planets. *Star systems* are other groupings of a star and orbiting planets.

The Structure of the Solar System

The great distances between objects in space makes it difficult to envision the entire solar system. Imagine trying to make a scale drawing of the sun and all eight planets. If you start with the sun as a one-centimeter circle in the center of the page, Earth would be one-tenth of a millimeter—hardly visible at all—more than a meter away!

3. *Absolute measurements* measure an exact distance or size. *Relative measurements* compare a size or distance to something else. Above, the sun is compared to a 1 cm circle. Why are relative size and distance useful for modeling the solar system?

Uranus and Neptune are difficult to see without the help of a telescope. The other planets in the solar system are easier to find among the many stars in the night sky. This photo shows Venus, Mars, and Jupiter over Utah. The planets do not emit light. They reflect light from the sun.

Another challenge is perspective. All objects in space are moving relative to each other. The entire solar system cannot be seen at the same time. Instead, scientists infer the structure by observing the motion of stars and planets over the course of a day and year. They also use telescopes, satellites, and space probes to study the solar system.

4. Think about trying to see a particular object in space. Which factors could affect whether or not you would be able to see the object? Circle all that apply.

   A. the brightness of the sky

   B. your position on Earth

   C. the brightness of the object

   D. the rotational speed of the object

The Sun Is the Center of the Solar System

The sun is the largest single object in the solar system. The sun is an average-sized star, yet it is large enough to contain 1.3 million Earth-sized planets! This large volume is filled with hot, churning hydrogen and helium, as well as trace amounts of many other elements such as oxygen, carbon, and iron. The sun has one-fourth the density of the Earth, but it is so large that it has 333,000 times more mass. An object's mass determines the strength of its gravitational field. The gravitational fields of stars are very strong and extend far into space. As a result, a star influences the motion of other objects around it. The sun lies at the center of the solar system. All other objects in the solar system exist at varying distances from the sun. The planets and other objects in the solar system are held in orbit by the mutual gravitational pull between themselves and the sun.

5. **Discuss** With a partner, develop a simple model that explains why the sun appears to move across the sky to an observer on Earth.

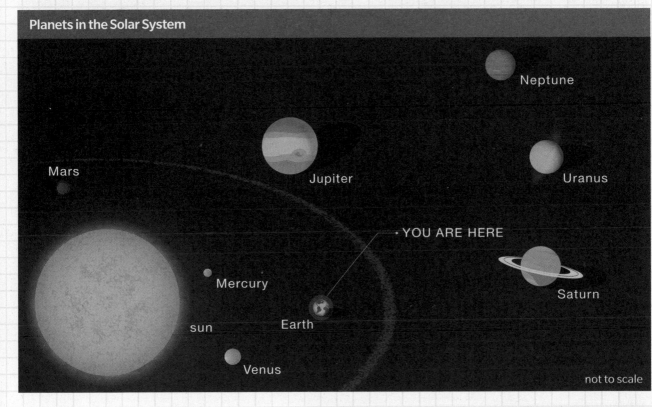

Planets in the Solar System

Neptune

Mars

Jupiter

Uranus

YOU ARE HERE

Mercury

Saturn

sun   Earth

Venus

not to scale

6. Analyze the data in the table. What are two categories that the planets could be sorted into based on the properties listed?

Planet	Diameter (km)	Density (g/cm³)	Distance from sun (millions of km)
Mercury	4,879	5.4	58
Venus	12,104	5.2	108
Earth	12,756	5.5	150
Mars	6,792	3.9	228
Jupiter	142,984	1.3	778
Saturn	120,536	0.68	1,433
Uranus	51,118	1.3	2,872
Neptune	49,528	1.6	4,495

Planets Orbit the Sun

The planets are the next largest category of objects in the solar system. The planets orbit the sun in the same direction. Each moves at a unique distance and speed. In addition to orbiting the sun, each planet also rotates on an axis. The planets can be divided into the inner, or terrestrial, planets (Mercury, Venus, Earth, and Mars), and the outer planets (gas giants Jupiter and Saturn and ice giants Uranus and Neptune).

Humans have directly observed and mapped planets and other objects in the night sky for thousands of years. All of these observations eventually led to a model of the solar system with the sun at the center. This model was supported by the observation that the planets move across the sky in a narrow band. This suggests that the planets are arranged in a disk shape around the sun. Scientists also observed that the planets orbit the sun in the same direction. This observation gives evidence for how the solar system may have formed.

The other seven planets in the solar system will be visible from Earth at the same time on May 6, 2492. This image shows how the planets will be aligned, based on a computer simulation. Notice how the planets are arranged in a narrow band.

7. How would you expect the pattern of planets in the sky to look if the solar system were not in a disk or plane? What shape would the pattern take?

EVIDENCE NOTEBOOK

8. Explain what observations would show that planets all move in the same direction around the sun. Record your evidence.

Moons and Other Small Bodies

The solar system includes many objects that are smaller than planets. Moons are rocky bodies that orbit larger bodies, such as planets, dwarf planets, and asteroids. Mercury and Venus are the only solar system planets without moons. Comets are chunks of dust and ice that orbit the sun. As comets approach the sun, they develop a glowing head and a long, thin tail of dust and gas. Asteroids are small rocky or metallic bodies that revolve around the sun in an area called the *asteroid belt*. It is found between the orbits of Mars and Jupiter. Meteoroids are bits of rocky or metallic space debris found throughout the solar system. Meteoroids are called meteors when they enter Earth's atmosphere. They collide with gases in the atmosphere and cause friction that generates heat and light.

9. This illustration of the solar system is not drawn to scale. Why do you think the artist decided not to draw the sizes and distances of the planets to scale?

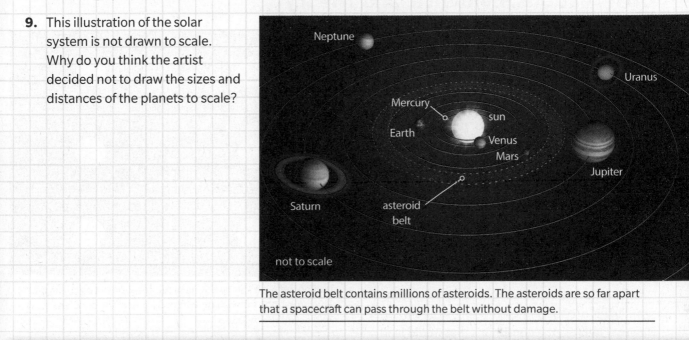

The asteroid belt contains millions of asteroids. The asteroids are so far apart that a spacecraft can pass through the belt without damage.

Measure the Solar System

Astronomical units (AUs) are used to measure distances in the solar system. One AU equals 149.6 million km, which is the average distance from the sun to Earth.

Planet	Distance from the sun (AU)
Mercury	0.4
Venus	0.7
Earth	1.0
Mars	1.5
Jupiter	5.2
Saturn	9.5
Uranus	19
Neptune	30

10. Look at the table showing the planetary distances from the sun. Which pattern can be seen in the table?

   A. All of the distances are less than double the preceding planetary distance, except the distance for Jupiter.

   B. The distances between the outer planets are smaller than the distances between the inner planets.

   C. All of the distances are three times the preceding planetary distance.

   D. All of the planets are an even number of AUs apart.

11. How does the gap between Mars and Jupiter support the idea that the asteroid belt contains material that failed to form a planet? If there were a planet between Mars and Jupiter, how many AUs would it be from the sun?

_____

_____

_____

Building a Hypothesis of How the Solar System Formed

Ancient astronomers used observations of the sky to develop the first models of Earth in space. As technology and science progressed, astronomers began to use telescopes to make observations of the solar system and beyond. Two important steps toward our modern understanding of the solar system took place in the 17th century.

Observations, Evidence, and Theory

Galileo was the first person known to use a telescope to observe the stars and planets. He supported the idea that Earth is not the center of the universe but that Earth and the other planets circle the sun. One of Galileo's most important discoveries was that Jupiter is a planet circled by four moons. His 1610 book, *The Sidereal Messenger*, included his drawings of Jupiter and its moons. Galileo thought that the way the moons orbited Jupiter was similar to the way the planets orbit the sun.

In 1687, Sir Isaac Newton published his theory that all matter in the universe attracted all other matter through a force he called *gravity*. His theory explained the motion of the planets around the sun. Gravity is the attractive force that keeps objects in orbit. In his orbital cannon thought experiment, Newton outlined the conditions that would lead to an object orbiting Earth. The same principles applied to objects orbiting the sun. Observations that provided evidence that the solar system consists of planets circling the sun and the theory of gravity were necessary for the next great leap in understanding the origin of the solar system.

12. Scientists study events in space, processes that occur beneath Earth's surface, and changes taking place on the deep ocean floor. How can scientists study what they cannot see or touch? How do you think they develop theories about these events?

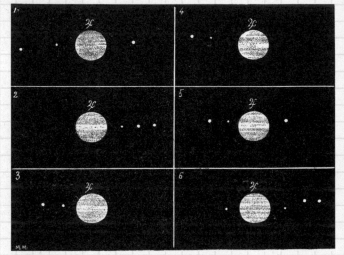

Galileo mapped the positions of Jupiter's moons every night. The large body in these drawings is Jupiter. The smaller bodies are the moons.

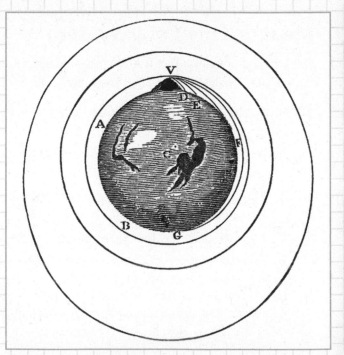

In Newton's thought experiment, a cannonball launched high above Earth at the right velocity would orbit Earth instead of falling to the ground or flying into space.

Kant's Nebular Hypothesis

In the mid-1700s, Immanuel Kant developed the nebular hypothesis of the origin of the solar system. He proposed that matter in the solar system began as separate particles. This cloud of dust and gas from which the planets and sun formed is now known as the **solar nebula.** Kant suggested that attractive forces between the particles caused them to collide and join together, forming larger clumps. As the clumps increased in size, their gravitational fields increased in strength, and they attracted even more particles. The sun formed at the middle of the cloud of particles, where the attractive forces were the greatest. The remaining particles joined with the larger masses until the planets were formed. The large mass of the sun and the gravitational attraction between the planets and the sun kept the planets in orbit around the sun. Kant's hypothesis explained the process in which matter in the solar system went from an unordered state to a structured system with distinct bodies orbiting the sun in a predictable pattern. While Kant's nebular hypothesis described the formation of the solar system, it did not explain several characteristics of the solar system. For example, his hypothesis did not explain why all planets orbit the sun in the same direction or why the planets orbit the sun in roughly the same plane.

13. **Draw** Storyboards can be drawn to illustrate the steps in a sequence. Use the space below to draw a storyboard that explains Kant's nebular hypothesis. Write a caption to support the art you make.

14. **Discuss** According to current criteria, a space object is classified as a planet if it (1) orbits a star, (2) is large enough to have a nearly spherical shape, and (3) has "cleared the neighborhood" around its orbit. The orbital path of a planet is cleared when smaller masses are attracted to and combine with the planet or are pushed to a different orbit. How is Kant's nebular hypothesis related to these criteria?

Laplace Refines Kant's Model

About 40 years after Kant's work became known, Pierre-Simon Laplace used mathematics to refine the nebular hypothesis. Laplace suggested that after forming in a collapsing cloud of dust and gas, the sun cooled and became more compact in size. This made the sun rotate more quickly. In the same way, ice skaters spin faster when they draw their arms into their bodies. For both the sun and the ice skater, the rotational speed increases as mass moves toward the center of the object.

Dust and gas were pushed outward while the sun's gravity pulled matter inward toward the sun. The constant push and pull flattened the cloud into a large disk. Scientists refer to these disks of matter as **protoplanetary disks.** The prefix "proto-" means "earliest" in Greek. The disk rotated around the sun, and material in the disk formed concentric rings of debris. Matter collided and fused in the rings, eventually forming the planets.

The ice skater begins to spin with her arms extended and her leg out. As she contracts her mass by bringing her arms and leg inward, she spins faster.

Laplace's Hypothesis of Solar System Formation

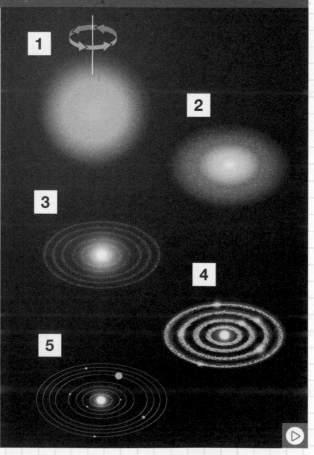

(1) A slowly rotating cloud of dust and gas **(2)** begins to condense, causing it to spin faster. The sun forms at the center of the cloud. **(3)** The cloud flattens into the shape of a disk, and rings of debris form in a plane. **(4)** Materials in each ring collide and clump together due to gravity, **(5)** forming planets and the solar system.

15. What aspects of the solar system are explained by Laplace's hypothesis of how the solar system formed? Circle all that apply.

   A. All planets orbit the sun in the same direction.

   B. Planets are dense collections of rock and gas with strong gravitational fields.

   C. Planets spin on their axes at very different rates.

   D. The orbital paths of the planets are arranged in a plane.

Hands-On Lab
Model Nebular Disk Formation

You will construct a model of nebular disk formation that is consistent with Laplace's hypothesis of solar system formation. Identify similarities and differences between the model and the formation of star systems in space.

Procedure

STEP 1 Use the compass to draw three separate circles on the tag board. Make one circle 3 cm in diameter. Make two circles 4 cm in diameter. Cut out the circles carefully using scissors.

STEP 2 Punch a hole in the center of each circle. For the 3 cm circle and one 4 cm circle, the hole should be just big enough to fit snugly over the dowel rod. For the other 4 cm circle, the hole should be slightly larger so that the circle can slide freely over the dowel.

STEP 3 Cut 8 strips of tag board that are 1.25 cm wide by 30 cm long.

STEP 4 Glue one end of each strip to the 4 cm circle that fits snugly over the dowel. Pinch and hold in place for 30–60 seconds. Space the strips evenly around the circle. Slide this circle over the dowel and glue it in place about 3 cm from the top of the dowel. Next, slide the 3 cm circle over the bottom of the dowel and glue it in position about 12 cm below the first circle. Give the glue time to dry.

STEP 5 Slide the remaining 4 cm circle over the bottom of the dowel. Glue the loose end of each strip to this circle, making sure the strips are evenly spaced. When the dowel is held upright, this circle should hang below the others and slide freely.

STEP 6 Hold the dowel upright between the palms of your hands. Predict what will happen when you spin the dowel by moving it between your palms. Record your prediction.

MATERIALS
- dowel rod, long and thin
- drawing compass
- glue
- hole punch
- pencil
- ruler
- scissors
- tag board

Cut along the lines to form the strips for the sphere.

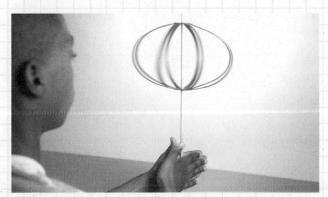
Glue the strips to the top and bottom tag board circles. Measure distances carefully.

Roll the dowel between both palms to control the spinning. Spin the dowel as fast as you can.

Analysis

STEP 7 Describe what you saw when you spun the dowel.

STEP 8 How does this model relate to the formation of the solar system? Include similarities and differences between the model and the formation of the solar system as described by Pierre-Simon Laplace.

Engineer It
Evaluate the Effect of Gravity

The planets are natural satellites that orbit the sun. The moon is a natural satellite that orbits Earth. Many artificial satellites also orbit Earth. Gravity keeps satellites in orbit around Earth, moons in orbit around planets, and planets and other objects in orbit around the sun. The organization of matter we observe on Earth, in the solar system, and in the universe would not exist without gravity.

16. What would happen to the satellites in orbit around Earth without gravity?

_____

_____

_____

_____

_____

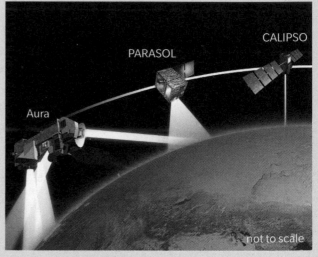

These satellites orbit Earth on a specific path and collect data related to climate change.

17. Brainstorm ways gravity could affect a space probe launched from Earth that is intended to travel to and orbit Jupiter. Why is it necessary to consider gravity when launching a spacecraft or putting a spacecraft into orbit?

_____

_____

_____

_____

Gathering Data on the Formation of Star Systems

In order to understand what is happening in a protoplanetary disk, astronomers develop models based on observations. This drawing is based on a model of star system formation. According to this model, the central star is surrounded by a large rotating disk of gas and dust. The central star is pulling in material from the outer disk. The arms of dust and gas form a bridge across the disk. Other material in the disk is forming clumps that will eventually form planets. By developing models like this one, astronomers are able to infer how the star system probably formed.

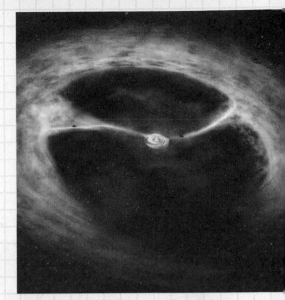

This artist's drawing shows a new star system forming in the disk surrounding a young star.

18. If the solar system formed similarly to this star system, what would you expect to see if you observed the sun? Would you expect to see it stationary or spinning?

Evidence of How Star Systems Form

The sun provides evidence of how the solar system formed. These illustrations show the changing positions of sunspots. Sunspots are dark patches that appear temporarily on the sun's surface.

19. What do you know about the sun's motion based on the nebular hypothesis model?

A. The sun and planets both move on the same orbital paths.

B. The sun rotates in the same direction as planets move around the sun.

C. The faster the sun moves, the faster the planets travel in their orbits.

D. There is no relationship between planetary movement and the sun.

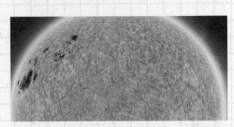

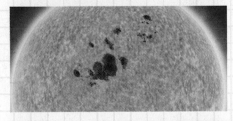

20. These images show the position of spots on the surface of the sun over a one-week period. Based on these images, what conclusion could you draw?

EVIDENCE NOTEBOOK

21. Explain the relationship between the sun's motion and the motion of the planets. Record your evidence.

Direct Observation of Star System Formation

The primary source of evidence supporting the hypothesis that the solar system formed from the solar nebula is the observation of similar processes occurring elsewhere in space. By using telescope technology, scientists can observe the formation of stars inside clouds of gas and dust. They can capture images of young stars surrounded by disks of debris. Some telescopes use electromagnetic radiation, such as x-rays, radio waves, gamma rays, and infrared light, to produce images of developing stars and their surroundings.

In recent years, astronomers and engineers have worked together to find evidence for the nebular hypothesis by looking for places elsewhere in the universe where new star systems are forming. Observing these events is costly. To share the costs and equipment, international science groups worked together to build the Atacama Large Millimeter Array (ALMA). ALMA is a series of 66 radio telescope dishes. The dishes work together to detect clouds of gas and dust like the solar nebula and other signs of star system formation such as protoplanetary disks. One of these disks that has been detected about 450 light-years away is shown in the illustration on the right.

Stars, and perhaps star systems, are forming within the Horsehead Nebula.

This illustration shows a protoplanetary disk. Objects like this can be observed using the Atacama Large Millimeter Array.

22. What stages of the nebular hypothesis do the images above represent? How do you know? Record your claim, evidence, and reasoning.

Computer Modeling and Simulations

Space telescopes do not provide images like those taken with a typical camera. The telescopes collect data, which is translated into an image by a computer. Sometimes artists or a computer program add color to these images. This helps people visualize the object or event being studied. Computers can also model phenomena in space. Models allow scientists to use physical and chemical laws to simulate events that are occurring in space. For example, scientists have modeled the formation of the solar system, the interaction between black holes, and even the collision of a planet and an asteroid.

Explore ONLINE!

This computer model shows dense areas of gas as bright areas in the cloud around a forming star.

23. Astronomers use models /experiments to represent space events that they cannot see directly or that occur over a long time span. Using computer models / current data / both models and data makes it possible to simulate the formation of the solar system. Computers allow scientists to perform investigations in accelerated / real time frames. This is important, because modeling the formation of the solar system on a 1:1 time scale would take billions / millions of years.

24. **Language SmArts** | **Write an Origin Story** You may have heard or read "origin stories." They often explain how a superhero gained certain powers. Choose the solar system, the sun, or a planet, and write an origin story about its formation. Include an illustration that clarifies important details in your story. Present your story and illustration to a classmate.

Additional Support for the Nebular Hypothesis

Several lines of evidence support the nebular hypothesis. These include the growing number of observations of forming star systems and the observation that the sun rotates in the same direction and plane in which the planets revolve. Other evidence supporting the nebular hypothesis includes computer models that explain why the inner planets of the solar system are composed of rock and metal while the outer planets are icy and gaseous. The evidence in support of the nebular hypothesis is so strong that the work of planetary astronomers today is to explain the details of how the solar system went from a cloud of gas and dust to the planets and other bodies seen today.

The Formation of Star Systems

By observing many stars at different stages, scientists have confirmed that stars follow a predictable life cycle. Stars form in nebulae that are dense and cold. When a nebula collapses, the temperature and pressure increase over time as particles in the nebula collide and clump together. A *protostar* forms at the center of the nebula, surrounded by gaseous and rocky debris.

Once the protostar becomes very hot (10 million Kelvin), it becomes a young star. The fusion of hydrogen into helium in the star generates large amounts of heat and light. As the young star warms, the core contracts and begins to spin. At this stage, the debris held by the star's gravity flattens into a protoplanetary disk, as described by Laplace in the nebular hypothesis. The early stages of planet formation occur in the bulging disk of matter surrounding the young star. Scientists have observed different stages of this process in many places throughout space. The results of computer modeling also support this part of the nebular hypothesis.

Particles collect into clumps due to the gravitational attraction between masses. The process increases in speed as the clumps get larger and the gravitational attraction increases.

25. If you sprinkle magnetic filings in a ring and then drag a magnet through the filings, the magnet will collect a cluster of filings. How is this a model for what happens in a protoplanetary disk?

    A. The magnet moves in an orbit in the same way that planets orbit the sun.

    B. As they move, the magnet and clumps of planetary matter both collect iron because of magnetism.

    C. The magnet collects iron filings as it moves around the ring just as a new planet collects smaller masses as it orbits its star.

    D. As they move, the magnet and clumps of planetary matter both collect matter due to their mass and gravity.

26. **Discuss** How does the magnet model differ from what occurs in a protoplanetary disk?

The Composition of the Planets

The nebular hypothesis describes how a cloud of dust and gas turned into a disk that eventually formed the sun, the planets, and all the objects in the solar system. The composition of planets in our solar system supports this hypothesis.

Over time, scientists used data gathered from telescopes and space probes to determine the properties of each planet. The inner planets (Mercury, Venus, Earth, and Mars) have rocky surfaces with features such as mountains, valleys, and craters. They also have few or no moons and molten metal cores. The outer planets (Jupiter, Saturn, Uranus, and Neptune) have thick atmospheres composed of hydrogen and helium. Only the center layers of these gas giants and ice giants are solid. Their large masses provide enough gravity to hold more moons than terrestrial planets.

not to scale

The difference in composition between the solar system's terrestrial planets and gas and ice giants provides evidence supporting the nebular hypothesis.

The temperature near the center of a protoplanetary disk would be very hot. Only elements that are solid at high temperatures would be able to form a solid planet near the center of the disk. This is why the inner, terrestrial, planets in the solar system consist of elements with high melting points. On the other hand, the outer planets in the solar system consist of elements with lower melting points, such as hydrogen. These elements became a significant part of the planets farther from the center of the disk.

27. Imagine you are an astronomer who recently discovered a star with a system of planets. What can you predict about the composition of planets closer to the star compared to planets farther from the star? Use evidence to support your claim.

EVIDENCE NOTEBOOK

28. Explain how the formation of the solar system caused the planets to orbit the sun in the same direction. Record your evidence.

The Nebular Theory

The nebular theory has become a widely accepted explanation for how the solar system formed. According to the nebular theory, nearby gravitational disturbances caused a large cloud of gas and dust to collapse into a space the size of the solar system. The mass of the nebula remained the same, but it occupied a much smaller space. The particles in the cloud collided and joined to form larger particles with more gravity. As a result of the collisions within the cloud, the nebula became very hot and began to spin. The collapsing and spinning caused the cloud to flatten into a disk shape. The hot, dense center of the cloud became the sun. The rest of the material formed concentric rings around the sun. The rings of material rotated in the same direction that the sun rotated. The material in the rings collided and clumped together until the largest pieces were the size of planets. Smaller objects, such as asteroids, meteoroids, and comets, are leftover debris that did not form into larger planets or moons. The planets orbit the sun because of the mutual attraction between the planets and the sun.

Do the Math

Graph the Density of the Planets

29. There are patterns apparent in the physical properties of the planets. Graph the planet densities in the space below. What pattern do you see?

_____

_____

30. The density of liquid water is 1.0 g/cm³. Add this information to your graph as a horizontal line. How does the graph help visualize the different types of materials that make up the planets?

_____

_____

_____

Planet	Density (g/cm³)
Mercury	5.4
Venus	5.2
Earth	5.5
Mars	3.9
Jupiter	1.3
Saturn	0.68
Uranus	1.3
Neptune	1.6

Continue Your Exploration

Name: _____ Date: _____

Check out the path below or go online to choose one of the other paths shown.

Careers in Science

- Hands-On Labs ✋
- Structure of Other Star Systems
- Propose Your Own Path

Go online to choose one of these other paths.

Conceptual Space Artist

Imagine using art and science together to inspire people and help them visualize things that we cannot see from Earth. This is what conceptual space artists do every day at the National Aeronautics and Space Administration (NASA). Scientists use various instruments to study space events, including instruments that collect data from space. Many of these instruments do not produce normal images. Instead, they collect data in various forms, including series of numbers or simple bands of colored light. Conceptual space artists turn these data into illustrations. This career requires an art background and the ability to use complex computer programs. The drawings and diagrams made by space artists help scientists and laypeople better understand space phenomena.

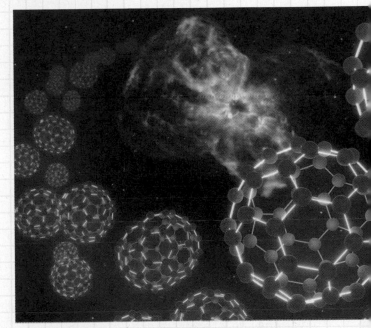

A space artist illustrated carbon spheres exiting a young nebula. Each carbon sphere has 60 carbon atoms arranged in a pattern similar to a soccer ball's.

This space artist's drawing shows what it might look like to watch three suns rising above the horizon from a moon that orbits HD188553 Ab, a large gaseous planet. It is based on data gathered by NASA's Keck telescope.

Continue Your Exploration

1. How is conceptual art different from a photograph?

2. Why are conceptual space artists important for astronomers and the public?

3. What is another example of a profession that translates scientific or professional information for a general audience?

4. **Collaborate** Working in a small group, select one type of space object (a star, nebula, galaxy, supernova, planet, or moon) and create a poster presenting the works of various conceptual space artists. Label each image with the title, artist's name (if available), the distance between the object and Earth, and the technology that provided data for the art.

Can You Explain It?

Name: _____   Date: _____

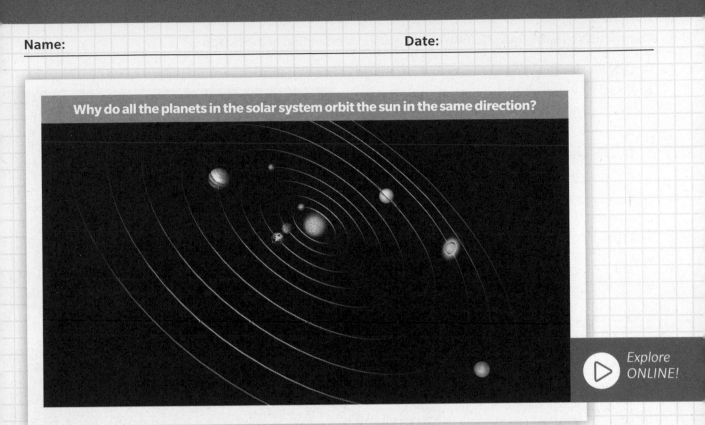

Why do all the planets in the solar system orbit the sun in the same direction?

Explore ONLINE!

EVIDENCE NOTEBOOK
Refer to the notes in your Evidence Notebook to help you construct an explanation for why all the planets orbit the sun in the same direction.

1. State your claim. Make sure your claim fully explains why all the planets in the solar system orbit the sun in the same direction.

2. Summarize the evidence you have gathered to support your claim and explain your reasoning.

Checkpoints

Answer the following questions to check your understanding of the lesson.

Use the illustration to answer Questions 3 and 4.

3. Which of these is most likely the next stage after the one shown in the illustration?

   A. a new star is formed

   B. the cloud of dust and gas begins to spin

   C. planets develop with individual orbits

   D. the disk flattens with the star at the center

4. When a new star contracts / expands, it begins to slow down / spin. As a result, the surrounding dust and gases compress into a sphere / disk.

Use the illustration to answer Questions 5 and 6.

5. Which stages involve the collision and clumping of matter in the nebula? Circle all that apply.

   A. stage 1

   B. stage 2

   C. stage 3

   D. stage 4

6. What evidence supporting the nebular hypothesis is shown?

   A. composition of the planets

   B. composition of the sun

   C. revolving disk of dust and gas

   D. direction of planet rotation

7. Why are there two different types of planets in the solar system?

   A. The amount of material available to form planets was greater in the outer reaches of the protoplanetary disk.

   B. Rocky material could not collect and form planets beyond the asteroid belt.

   C. The nebular cloud from which the solar system formed had very little gas.

   D. The sun's heat allowed only rocky planets to form in the inner portion of the solar system.

Interactive Review

Complete this section to review the main concepts of the lesson.

The solar system contains the sun, planets, and many smaller bodies.

A. Describe the patterns that early observers noticed in the movements of bodies in space.

The nebular hypothesis of solar system formation explains how the solar system formed from the gas and dust of a nebula and why all planets orbit the sun in the same direction.

B. How was the nebular hypothesis of solar system formation refined to account for the motion of the planets?

Scientists have gathered a variety of evidence to support the nebular hypothesis, including the connection between solar system formation and the composition of the planets.

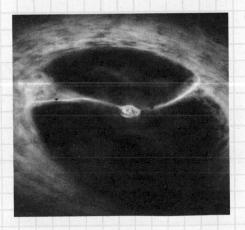

C. What lines of evidence support the nebular theory of solar system formation?

Earth and the Solar System

The sun shines through the center gap in Stonehenge in England. This marks the summer solstice, the longest day of the year.

By the end of this lesson . . .

you will be able to use evidence to explain the current scientific model of Earth's place in the solar system.

Go online to view the digital version of the Hands-On Lab for this lesson and to download additional lab resources.

CAN YOU EXPLAIN IT?

What are "shooting stars"?

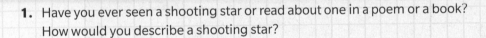

For thousands of years people have watched "shooting stars" streak across the sky. Showers of shooting stars occur at regular times each year. However, shooting stars do not follow the normal movement of stars through the night sky. They appear as a streak of light and disappear moments later.

Explore ONLINE!

1. Have you ever seen a shooting star or read about one in a poem or a book? How would you describe a shooting star?

2. What conditions are necessary to see a shooting star?

EVIDENCE NOTEBOOK As you explore the lesson, gather evidence to help explain why shooting stars behave differently than other stars do.

Observing the Sky and the Solar System

The Sky in Motion

Throughout human history, people have watched the sky. The sun rose and set and marked the days and nights. The moon passed through phases from full to new and back to full. The moon's cycle determined the months in a year. People studied the sky and mapped the stars. They noted how stars appeared to move. They watched, recorded, and constructed explanations of the patterns that occurred through the days, months, and years. These observations became the foundations of astronomy.

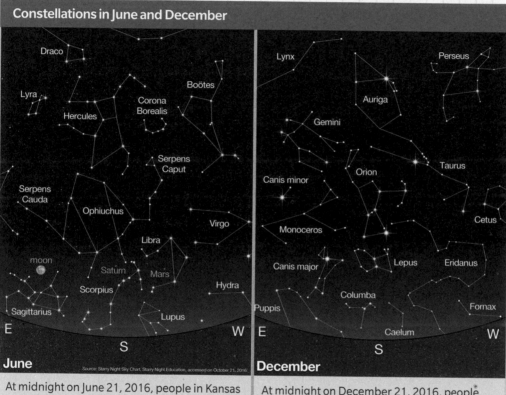

Constellations in June and December

June

Source: Starry Night Sky Chart, Starry Night Education, accessed on October 21, 2016

December

At midnight on June 21, 2016, people in Kansas could see the constellations Scorpius, Libra, and Sagittarius, as well as the planets Saturn and Mars.

At midnight on December 21, 2016, people in Kansas could see the constellations Canis Major, Canis Minor, and Orion, among others.

The Seasonal Stars

Early astronomers looked at the night sky with only their unaided eyes. As they mapped the visible stars, they noticed that some stars seemed to form patterns or shapes. These stars also appeared to move across the sky as a unit, called a *constellation*.

　　Although the stars of constellations stayed together, the constellations themselves moved across the night sky. They rose from the eastern horizon and set in the west, much like the sun and moon rose and set. Some stars, such as Polaris, and constellations, such as Ursa Major, were visible all year. Other stars and constellations appeared during different seasons. Astronomers observed that the seasonal star patterns repeated year after year. Early scientists and philosophers developed explanations for these regular movements of objects in the sky.

3. **Discuss** How do you think the observation of different constellations in different seasons was explained by people who thought Earth did not move at all? Explain your reasoning.

The Wandering Stars

Some stars did not appear to behave like the other stars. They would rise and set along with the rest of the stars. However, when observed over several weeks, they appeared to change their location among the other stars. Greek astronomers called those bodies *astéres planétai*, or "wandering stars." They are the planets we can easily see from Earth: Mercury, Venus, Mars, Jupiter, and Saturn. As planets moved across the sky, they traveled at different speeds. Sometimes, a planet would catch up to and pass another object that appeared to move more slowly. As they moved, planets appeared to pass in front of or behind the sun or other planets. When plotted on a sky chart for days or weeks, some planets' paths through the sky appeared to loop or move backward. This reverse motion puzzled astronomers. They struggled to construct an explanation for this phenomenon.

Language SmArts
Interpret Words and Visuals

4. Look at the terms and the meanings of their root words. Then create a label for each image by matching the term to the correct image.

Term	Root meanings
retrograde	Latin roots: *retro-* means "backward" and *gradi* means "to walk or step"
transit	Latin root: *transire* means "to cross"

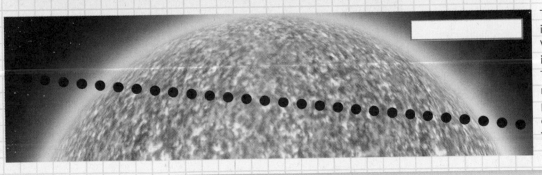

not to scale

Mars appears to move backward or have a looping path as its movement is viewed from Earth over several weeks.

This composite image shows Venus as it passes in front of the sun. The dark circles represent the positions of Venus over several hours.

5. From Earth, the moon is seen to transit in front of both the sun and Venus. Venus transits across the sun. List the three bodies described in order of increasing distance from Earth. Explain your thinking.

Early Models of the Solar System

Early astronomers developed models of the solar system based on what they knew. Because objects in the sky appeared to circle Earth, many astronomers placed Earth at the center of the model. The well-known Greek philosopher Aristotle (384–322 BCE) developed a model that had a fixed, non-moving Earth as the center of the universe. He proposed that all other bodies in the sky—including the moon, the sun, the planets, and the stars—moved around Earth. Aristotle claimed that all objects in the sky moved along regular, perfectly circular paths. This *geocentric*, or Earth-centered, model explained why objects in the sky appear to revolve around Earth on regular paths. It explained why Earth appears—to someone on Earth's surface—to be unmoving. It also explained why certain planets would transit across others.

6. Which of the following observations support Aristotle's geocentric model? Select all statements that apply.

  A. The sun, moon, and stars appear to follow a circular path through the sky.

  B. The sun and moon appear to be the same size and brightness as the stars.

  C. The sun, moon, and stars seem to move at the same rate across the sky.

  D. For people on Earth, the planet does not feel like it is moving.

  E. Some planets appear to cross between the sun and Earth.

  F. Some planets appear to pass behind and beyond the sun.

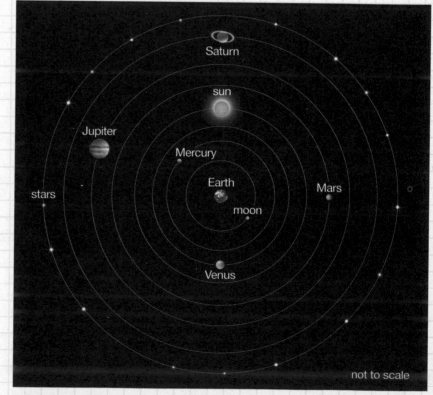

In Aristotle's model of the universe, the planets, sun, moon, and stars all revolved around a fixed, non-moving Earth.

Parallax and Geocentrism

To understand another argument for the geocentric model, it is important to understand a phenomenon called parallax. **Parallax** is the apparent shift in position of an object when it is viewed from different points. As an example, look at the photos that demonstrate parallax. Parallax can be used to measure the distance to an object based on the size of the apparent shift in position when the object is viewed from two places. The bigger the apparent shift in position is, the closer the object is to the viewer.

      The stars and constellations do not appear to change positions relative to each other when viewed from Earth with an unaided eye. Astronomers reasoned that this fact indicated that either the stars are extremely far away or they are unmoving. Aristotle's geocentric model proposed that the stars were fixed in position on a sphere that orbited Earth. This explanation fit the evidence, so it was accepted by other astronomers.

7. What would Aristotle's geocentric model predict about the brightness of the planets when viewed from different places on Earth? What about the stars? Explain your reasoning.

Ptolemy Answers the Retrograde Motion Problem

Aristotle's model failed to explain retrograde motion of planets or strange phenomena like shooting stars or comets. About 400 years after Aristotle, Claudius Ptolemy improved Aristotle's model by explaining retrograde motion. He claimed that planets moved in small circles, called *epicycles,* along their orbits around Earth. As the planets moved on these epicycles, they sometimes appeared to move backward. Ptolemy's geocentric model was accepted by most scientists for about 1,000 years.

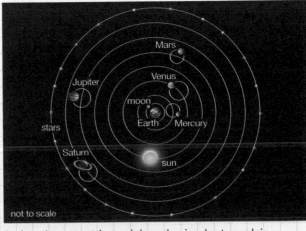

Ptolemy's geocentric model used epicycles to explain retrograde motion.

Hands-On Lab
Investigate Parallax

Use parallax to compare the relative distances between objects.

Procedure

MATERIALS
- markers (4 colors)
- meterstick
- pushpin (at least 10 mm tall)
- sticky notes
- stool or chair
- table
- tape

STEP 1 Place the table about 2 m from the wall. Tape the meterstick to the table so that the 100 cm mark is closest to the wall.

STEP 2 Place the pushpin into the meterstick at 100 cm. Sit or kneel on the side of the table farthest from the wall. Place the tip of your nose on the 0 cm end of the meterstick. Make sure you are positioned so that your eyes are evenly spaced on opposite sides of the meterstick.

STEP 3 Without moving your head, close your right eye. Tell your partner where the pin appears against the background. He or she will mark that point on the wall with a labeled sticky note.

STEP 4 Without moving your head, switch your opened and closed eyes. Tell your partner where the pin appears on the grid paper. He or she will mark that point with a labeled sticky note.

STEP 5 Repeat Steps 4–6 with the pushpin at 75 cm, 50 cm, and 25 cm. Make sure your head is in the same position, with the tip of your nose on the 0 cm end, for all four placements of the pushpin.

Analysis

STEP 6 What pattern did you see between the distance between the pin and your nose and the distance between the apparent positions of the pin when viewed with alternating eyes?

STEP 7 Stars do not appear to change positions when parallax is used to view them from Earth's surface with the unaided eye. How do you think this evidence supported ancient astronomers' belief in early geocentric models?

Analyze Data That Do Not Fit the Model

Aristotle's and Ptolemy's models included stars and planets that moved at a constant rate. The stars did not change their relative positions or brightnesses. These models explained events that fit a pattern. However, ancient astronomers from around the world recorded some events that did not appear to fit the observed patterns of motion of objects in the sky. Resolving these events with existing models of the universe became a challenge for all astronomers.

Observed phenomenon	Description
	In 1572, a bright new star (*Nova Stella*) appeared in the constellation Cassiopeia. This object did not change position relative to the other stars, so it was not a planet. It faded from sight two years later.
	Sometimes objects appeared among the stars, glowing faintly at first then getting brighter and larger over time. These objects had a bright "head" with streaming "tails" behind them. They were visible at night for several weeks to a few months, and they slowly changed position relative to the horizon and the background stars. Then, the objects faded away.
	Shooting stars appeared and moved across the sky in only a few seconds. They moved in every direction, even opposite the direction of the background stars. Some exploded in the sky, creating a thunderous boom and sending shock waves toward Earth's surface. Some of these objects even impacted Earth's surface.

8. Explain the similarities and differences between the observations that supported the geocentric models of the solar system and the phenomena described in the table.

_____

_____

9. Imagine that a small, bright object appeared in the sky, moved along with a nearby constellation, and then disappeared a year later. Scientists in China, Persia, Europe, and Central America observed the event. Where did this phenomenon most likely occur? How do you know?

_____

_____

EVIDENCE NOTEBOOK

10. Some people believe that shooting stars are stars that fell from the sky. What evidence do you have that supports or contradicts this belief?

Incorporating New Discoveries

Despite the widespread acceptance of the geocentric model, astronomers continued to gather data and refine the model. Many Indian and Arab astronomers made great advances in mathematic models that explained the movements of objects in the solar system. In 1543, a scientist named Nicolaus Copernicus used their calculations to propose a new model of the solar system: one with the sun at the center. Copernicus's *heliocentric*, or sun-centered, model explained retrograde motion in a simpler way. It relied on the sun being at the center and the planets arranged around the sun based on how quickly each planet orbits the sun.

11. Discuss Why might scientists favor Copernicus's heliocentric model over Ptolemy's geocentric model?

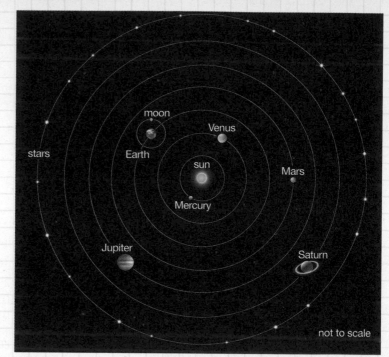

Copernicus's heliocentric model of the solar system put each planet, including Earth, in orbit around the sun. The moon orbited Earth.

Revising and Expanding the Model

In the late 1500s, Danish scientist Tycho Brahe built huge instruments that allowed him to take extremely precise measurements of stars and planets. His assistant, Johannes Kepler, used Brahe's data to calculate the shapes of planetary orbits. By suggesting that planets have elliptical, or oval-shaped, orbits rather than circular orbits, Kepler was able to explain complex planetary motions. These new findings helped convince scientists that Earth and the other planets revolve around the sun.

Tycho Brahe's Observatory

New Technology Led to New Discoveries

As Kepler was publishing his work, revolutionary technologies were being developed. In Italy, Galileo Galilei combined two magnifying lenses to make the first telescope in 1609. A **telescope** is an instrument that collects and concentrates light from distant objects to make the objects appear larger or brighter. Early telescopes magnified objects by only three to 30 times. But that small amount had a huge effect on astronomy.

Galileo's observations through his telescopes revealed details of planets and moons that changed centuries of scientific thought. He noticed that the surface of Earth's moon was rugged, not smooth. He observed sunspots on the sun and identified the phases of Venus. He also saw four small objects moving around Jupiter. These moons of Jupiter would finally prove that objects could orbit bodies other than Earth.

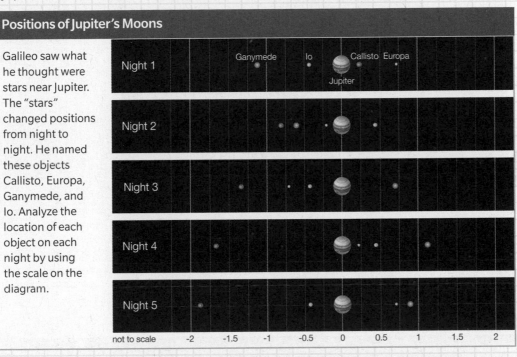

Positions of Jupiter's Moons

Galileo saw what he thought were stars near Jupiter. The "stars" changed positions from night to night. He named these objects Callisto, Europa, Ganymede, and Io. Analyze the location of each object on each night by using the scale on the diagram.

12. Look at the diagram. Which object appeared to move the fastest? Which object appeared to move the slowest? Explain your reasoning.

13. Use the scale on the diagram to determine the maximum distance each object travels away from Jupiter. Place that number in the center column of the chart. Then rank the objects in order of increasing distance from Jupiter.

Object	Maximum distance from Jupiter on the scale	Rank by distance from Jupiter (1 = closest and 4 = farthest)
Callisto		
Europa		
Ganymede		
Io		

A Growing Family of Objects

Advancements in telescopes occurred quickly over the next 300 to 400 years. Each advancement allowed scientists to see farther or with greater clarity and detail. Scientists collected data and used mathematical modeling to discover and describe new planets, moons, and numerous smaller objects in the solar system.

Mathematical models predicted that planets should exist beyond the orbit of Saturn and between Mars and Jupiter. Scientists used telescopes to look for these predicted objects. In 1871, the planet Uranus was discovered beyond Saturn's orbit. In 1801, a small, round object was discovered between the orbits of Mars and Jupiter. This object, named Ceres, was not a planet. It was the first object identified in the asteroid belt and is now considered a dwarf planet. The planet Neptune was discovered in 1846, and the dwarf planet Pluto was discovered in 1930.

Today, both ground-based telescopes, such as the South African Large Telescope (SALT), and space telescopes, such as the Hubble Space Telescope, gather data that show distant galaxies, newly forming solar systems, and the birth and death of stars.

14. New technologies, such as astrolabes / telescopes, allowed astronomers to see dim or distant objects in space. The development of new technology is necessary / unnecessary to the advancement of science. Scientists must consider / disregard new evidence as they create explanations for observed phenomena.

EVIDENCE NOTEBOOK

15. Use the following information about small bodies in the solar system to record evidence that might help you identify the source of shooting stars.

Small Bodies in the Solar System

Moons and dwarf planets in this illustration are shown roughly to scale. The smaller objects, such as meteoroids, would be invisible at that scale, so they are shown in an enlarged view.

meteoroid   asteroid   comet   dwarf planet   moon

not to scale

Moons are bodies that orbit larger bodies such as planets, dwarf planets, or asteroids, not the sun. Some moons are round, such as Earth's moon. Many moons are not round and may be asteroids or other space debris that are captured by the gravity of the larger body they orbit around.

Dwarf planets are similar to planets. They orbit the sun, and they are large enough to be roughly spherical. However, dwarf planets have not cleared their orbit of other large objects. Most dwarf planets are in areas that are surrounded by many small and large objects, such as asteroids and other dwarf planets.

Comets are small bodies of ice, rock, and dust. They follow highly elliptical orbits around the sun. As a comet passes close to the sun, gas and dust break off of the comet and form tails.

Asteroids are small, irregularly shaped rocky and metallic bodies. They range from the size of a car to several kilometers across. Although most asteroids orbit the sun in the asteroid belt (between the orbits of Mars and Jupiter), some travel through space on elliptical orbits like comets. They cross the orbits of other bodies, including Earth.

Meteoroids are small, rocky or metallic bodies. They may be debris left over from when the solar system formed. They may also break off of comets or asteroids. If a meteoroid enters Earth's atmosphere, it burns up. The short, bright streak of light is called a *meteor*.

Compare and Categorize Solar System Objects

Objects in our solar system are categorized according to their observable characteristics. For example, astronomers use size, shape, and orbit to classify objects. Planets are spherical and orbit the sun. Moons may be spherical or irregular, and they orbit larger bodies, such as planets, dwarf planets, or asteroids. Knowing the characteristics of space objects helps astronomers classify new objects that are discovered.

Observed Objects in the Solar System				
Body	**Shape**	**Orbits**	**Orbited by**	**Orbit cleared**
Ceres	sphere	sun	––	No
Ida	irregular	sun	Dactyl	No
Mercury	sphere	sun	––	Yes
Neptune	sphere	sun	14 bodies	Yes
Phobos	irregular	Mars	––	––
Pluto	sphere	sun	Charon	No
Titan	sphere	Saturn	––	––
Vesta	irregular	sun	––	No

16. Identify whether each object listed is a planet, dwarf planet, asteroid, or moon. Write the name of each object in the correct column.

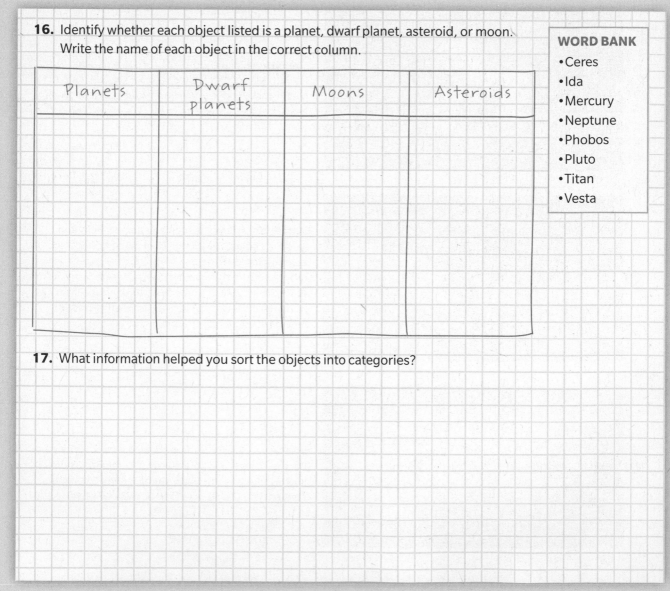

Planets	Dwarf planets	Moons	Asteroids

WORD BANK
- Ceres
- Ida
- Mercury
- Neptune
- Phobos
- Pluto
- Titan
- Vesta

17. What information helped you sort the objects into categories?

Exploring the Solar System with Models

Mathematical modeling is important in determining the structure of the solar system. One important part of mathematical modeling is scale. *Scale* is the mathematical relationship between the measurements or distances in a model and the actual measurements or distances of an object or system. It is difficult to imagine distances as large as those in space. Scale provides a way to compare such distances accurately.

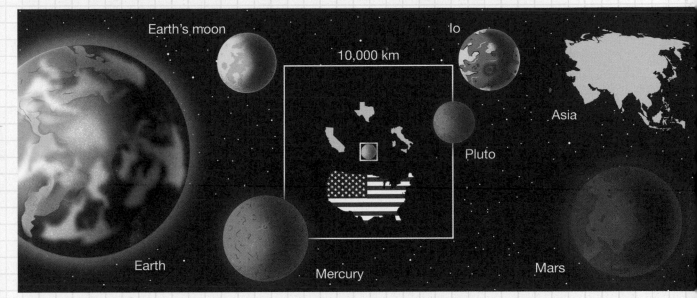

Scale lets us compare familiar objects and distances to astronomical objects and distances. For example, the diameter of Mercury is about the distance across the United States, and the diameter of Mars is about the distance across the continent of Asia.

18. Why would a scientist want to make a scale model of the solar system? Identify at least three ways scale could help someone understand the solar system.

Size and Distance in the Solar System

Models compare various characteristics of different objects. There are many ways to model the solar system. A physical model or a visual model, such as a drawing or map, could show the structure of the solar system. A mathematical model or a computer model could describe how objects in the solar system move.

Some models are made to scale. Some are not. Both scale and not-to-scale models can be useful. The type of model used depends on what information needs to be shown and how that information is being presented. Some aspects of the solar system are difficult to show with scale models. It is easy to make a scale model of the size of the sun and planets. Adding small asteroids and space dust to that scale model is more challenging. Modeling the huge distances between objects in space is also difficult.

Hands-On Lab
Model the Solar System

Scientists measure distances inside the solar system using kilometers or astronomical units. One **astronomical unit** (AU) is the average distance from the sun to Earth, about 150 million km. Create a scale model of the sun and planets and the distances between them.

Procedure and Analysis (Part 1)

STEP 1 Look at the table called *Solar System Objects*. The table lists the diameter (in km) of the sun and each planet. Use the numbers 1–9 to rank the sun and planets in order from the largest to the smallest.

STEP 2 Look at the objects available for your model. Compare their relative sizes. Predict which objects could be used to represent the sun and each planet in a scaled model of the solar system. Write your responses in the table.

STEP 3 Measure and record the diameter of each object.

Solar System Objects				
Solar system object	Diameter (km)	Relative size (biggest = 1, smallest = 9)	Representative object in model	Diameter of object (cm)
Sun	1,392,000	1		
Mercury	4,879	9		
Venus	12,104			
Earth	12,756			
Mars	6,792			
Jupiter	142,984			
Saturn	120,536			
Uranus	51,118			
Neptune	49,528			

STEP 4 The dwarf planet Ceres has a diameter of 930 km. Analyze the scale properties of the objects in your model to determine which object would best represent Ceres in the model: a pinhead (1 mm), a baseball (75 mm), a grain of salt (0.3 mm), or a table tennis ball (30 mm). Explain your reasoning.

Procedure and Analysis (Part 2)

STEP 1 To use the same scale for distance in the solar system as you used for size, find the distance of 1 AU at this scale. Remember that the sun is 1,392,000 km in diameter and 1 AU (Earth's distance from the sun) is about 150,000,000 km. Divide the distance of 1 AU in km by the diameter of the sun in km to find out how many solar diameters are in one AU. Then multiply by the diameter of the model sun (in cm) to see how far 1 AU should be in the model.

$$\frac{1 \text{ AU (in km)}}{\text{sun's diameter (in km)}} \times \text{model sun diameter (in cm)} = \text{length of 1 AU in model}$$

STEP 2 Divide the answer in cm by 100 to get the answer in meters. The meter is a convenient unit; one meter is about the length of one very long stride.

STEP 3 Fill in the table below to show how far from the sun each planet should be placed in your model. Round answers to the nearest meter.

Approximate Distances from the Sun to the Planets			
Solar system object	Distance from sun (km)	Distance from sun (AU)	Distance from sun in model (m)
Mercury	58,000,000	0.4	
Venus	108,000,000	0.7	
Earth	150,000,000	1.0	
Mars	228,000,000	1.5	
Jupiter	778,000,000	5.2	
Saturn	1,433,000,000	9.5	
Uranus	2,872,000,000	19	
Neptune	4,495,000,000	30	

STEP 4 Place the model sun in one corner of the room. Place as many planets as you can the correct distance from the sun, using the same scale for distance as for size. How many planets will fit in your classroom?

STEP 5 Some people have said that "There is a huge amount of space in space!" What do you think they mean by that?

STEP 6 **Engineer It** Is it possible for one model to accurately show both the size of the planets and sun and the distance between the planets and sun? Describe the trade-offs between developing a model that illustrates both accurately and developing a model that illustrates only one of the measurements accurately.

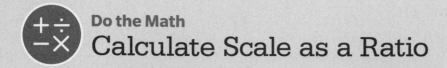

Do the Math

Calculate Scale as a Ratio

Scale is often expressed as a ratio. A ratio is a way of comparing the relationship of quantity, amount, or size between two numbers. For example, the solar system has eight planets and one star (the sun). Thus, the ratio of planets to stars in the solar system is 8 to 1, or 8:1.

To calculate the scale of a model of the solar system, divide the actual size of a body by the size of the object that represents that same body in the model. The same process can be used to determine the scale for distances. The answer will be a ratio of the actual units to the units in the model. This is commonly expressed as "1 (unit in the model)" to "X (actual units)" or "1:X." For example, the miniature town is built on a scale of 1:25. In other words, every 1 m in the model equals 25 m in the real town.

Scale, expressed as a ratio, can be used to make detailed models. The miniature town in this photo was built to scale with the real town. Every streetlight, tree, and building is exactly in proportion with its real-life counterpart.

19. Find the scale ratio that you used to model the solar system. Remember that one AU is about 150,000,000 kilometers, which is represented by 22 meters in the model. What is the scale of the model represented by a ratio?

20. How does using ratios or other mathematical comparisons help scientists communicate information?

Continue Your Exploration

Name: _____   **Date:** _____

Check out the path below or go online to choose one of the other paths shown.

People in Science

- **Hands-On Labs** ✋
- **Engineer It: Reflecting and Refracting Telescopes**
- **Propose Your Own Path**

Go online to choose one of these other paths.

Contributions of Indian and Arab Astronomers

Between 700 and 1500 CE, Indian and Arab scientists made remarkable advances in astronomy while Europe experienced the Dark Ages. In the 8th century CE, Indian mathematician Brahmagupta developed mathematical formulas that he used to calculate the rising and setting of the sun and moon and the timing of solar and lunar eclipses. His work was studied by many astronomers and mathematicians throughout the Middle East.

In the early 9th century CE, Arab mathematician Muhammad ibn Musa al-Khwarizmi invented the quadrant, a tool for determining the angle of elevation to the sun and the North Star. Al-Khwarizmi also used algebra to determine the positions of the sun, moon, and five known planets at specific times of the day, month, and year.

During this time, Arab scientists improved an instrument called an astrolabe. Astronomers used this tool to locate stars and planets in the sky. It could also be used to tell time and to identify latitude for navigation. Arab astronomers also calculated that a solar year, or how long Earth takes to orbit the sun, lasts 365 days, 5 hours, 46 minutes, and 24 seconds. Some Arab and Indian astronomers also suggested a heliocentric model of the solar system.

By 1437, astronomers at the observatory at Samarkand had cataloged the location and movement of 992 stars. Many stars on today's star maps still bear Arab names, including Rigel, Aldebaran, Deneb, and Betelgeuse.

An astrolabe such as this one was used to accurately determine the positions of the sun and stars.

The observatory at Samarkand recorded the positions and movements of 992 stars.

Continue Your Exploration

1. How do advances made by Arab astronomers affect the science of astronomy today? Circle all that apply.

   A. Modern astronomers identify stars by the names or positions cataloged by astronomers in Arab observatories more than 1,000 years ago.

   B. Instruments developed or improved by Arab astronomers impacted discoveries made by European astronomers centuries later.

   C. The geocentric model of the solar system was supported by mathematical models and observations made by Arab astronomers.

   D. The modern annual calendar is based on the length of time Earth takes to revolve around the sun.

2. Which long-ago Arab scientific contributions are still used today?

3. Arab and Indian astronomers developed mathematical formulas / historic records and updated and invented technology like telescopes / astrolabes. These contributions changed the science of astronomy by providing more precise data / clearer views of objects in the sky.

4. **Collaborate** Working with a partner, develop an illustrated timeline that covers Indian and Arab contributions to astronomy during Europe's Dark Ages. Prepare a presentation of your work for the class. Be sure to identify advances in solar system science made possible by improved engineering and advances in engineering made possible by advances in science and mathematics.

Can You Explain It?

Name: _____   **Date:** _____

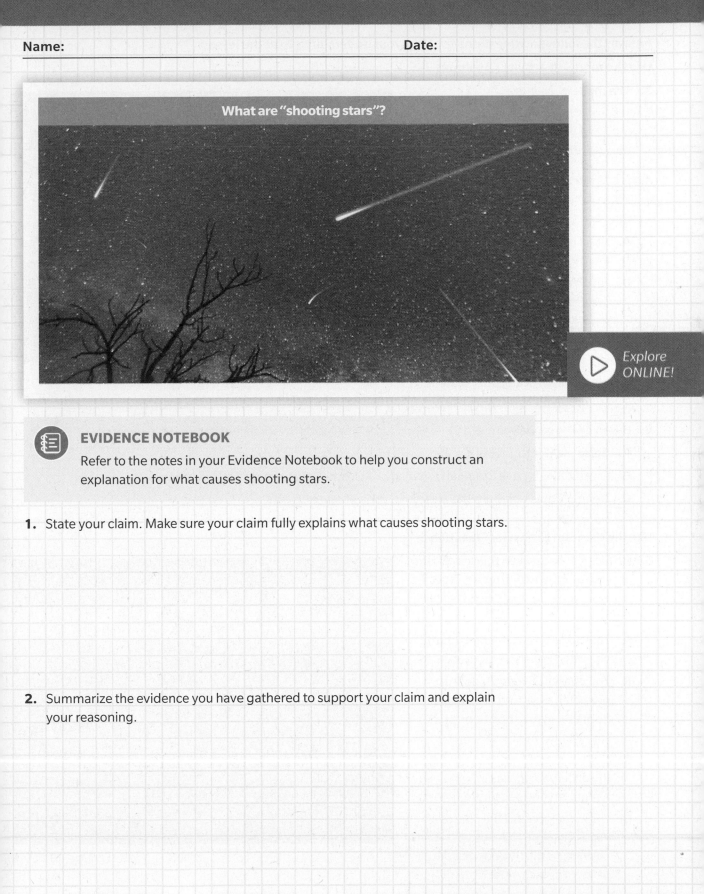

What are "shooting stars"?

Explore ONLINE!

EVIDENCE NOTEBOOK

Refer to the notes in your Evidence Notebook to help you construct an explanation for what causes shooting stars.

1. State your claim. Make sure your claim fully explains what causes shooting stars.

2. Summarize the evidence you have gathered to support your claim and explain your reasoning.

Checkpoints

Answer the following questions to check your understanding of the lesson.

Use the model to answer Questions 3–5.

3. The model presents a heliocentric / geocentric model of the solar system in which all objects orbit Earth / the sun.

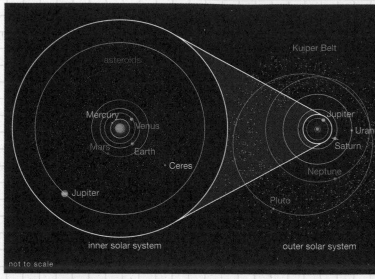

4. Is this model to scale regarding the sizes of the planets and distances between them? Why or why not?

   A. Yes. That is why the outer planets are shown in a separate box.

   B. No. The distances in the solar system are too great to produce a model accurate to distance that still has inner planets visible.

   C. No. The outer planet distances are drawn to scale, but the inner planets need to be drawn farther from the sun to be visible.

5. Based on the model, why are Ceres and Pluto classified as dwarf planets rather than planets?

   A. Ceres and Pluto are both round.

   B. Dwarf planets have irregularly shaped orbits, and planets have elliptical orbits.

   C. Neither Ceres nor Pluto has cleared its orbit of other objects.

Use the diagram to answer Question 6.

6. How can the observed phases of Venus provide evidence to support a specific model of the solar system? Select all that apply.

   A. The model that better predicts the phases is likely to be more accurate.

   B. The phases of Venus follow a predictable pattern that results from the relative positions of the sun, Venus, and Earth.

   C. Neither model accurately predicts the observed phases of Venus, so neither model is accurate.

   D. The models predict the phases of Venus differently because the relative positions of the three bodies are different in each model.

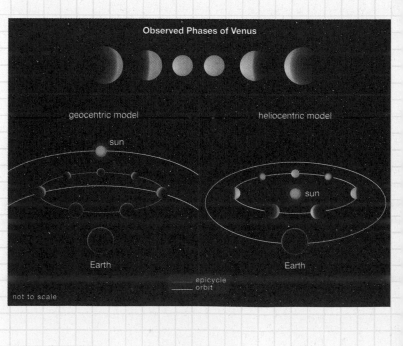

Interactive Review

Complete this section to review the main concepts of the lesson.

For thousands of years, scientists have used the movements of the sun, moon, and stars to develop models of Earth's place in the universe.

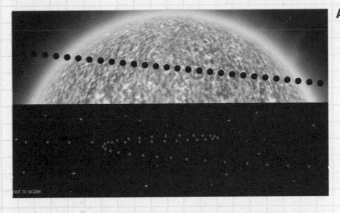

A. Outline the types of evidence that scientists used to develop early models of the solar system.

Mathematical models and the invention of telescopes changed and expanded scientists' ideas about the solar system and universe.

B. How did the telescope bring about changes in astronomy?

A scale model can be used to compare the sizes and distances between objects in space.

C. Explain how using scale helps scientists model different sizes or distances in the solar system.

Earth's Place in the Universe

This photo shows a star forming near the edge of the Milky Way galaxy. It was taken by the Hubble Space Telescope.

By the end of this lesson . . .

you will be able to explain how scientists use data and models to determine the structure of galaxies and the universe.

Go online to view the digital version of the Hands-On Lab for this lesson and to download additional lab resources.

CAN YOU EXPLAIN IT?

How can we make a model of the Milky Way galaxy that shows Earth's location?

Earth is a small planet close to one star, the sun. The sun is one of billions of stars in the Milky Way galaxy. This is an artist's conception of how the Milky Way would look from a distance.

1. If you were standing on a sidewalk, how could you figure out where you are in a city without using a map?

2. How would a map of a galaxy be different from a map of a city?

EVIDENCE NOTEBOOK As you explore this lesson, gather evidence to explain how scientists determine Earth's location within the Milky Way galaxy.

Modeling the Milky Way

Our galaxy, the Milky Way, is just one out of billions of galaxies. A **galaxy** is a large collection of stars, gas, and dust that is held together by gravity. Most of the Milky Way is not visible when we observe space. Over time, astronomers developed technologies that expanded our ability to observe objects in space. Telescopes and space probes can be used to collect data and give us a much better understanding of our galaxy. These data also expand our understanding of the size of our galaxy compared to the surrounding universe. The **universe** includes space and all of the energy and matter within it.

The Milky Way is easier to see from remote areas. City lights interfere with light from space.

3. **Discuss** How do scientific discovery and technology influence each other?

The Milky Way in the Night Sky

For much of human history, the Milky Way was a mystery. Some civilizations thought it was a flowing river. Others thought it was milk spilled by gods that lived far above Earth. Greek philosophers debated whether it was a band of faint stars or something glowing within Earth's atmosphere. When Persian astronomers observed that larger bodies (planets) would pass in front of the glowing band, they theorized that the Milky Way was a collection of many distant stars. However, without the ability to distinguish individual stars within the band, they could not confirm this hypothesis.

The Milky Way galaxy can only be seen in a very clear and dark sky and appears as a hazy band of clouds.

The Milky Way through a Telescope

When Galileo Galilei first used a telescope to observe the Milky Way in the early 1600s, he described the Milky Way as a collection of "innumerable stars distributed in clusters." Later astronomers made observations of the Milky Way from different locations on Earth. Over time, it became clear that the Milky Way surrounds Earth and the sun. Our solar system is a part of the Milky Way, not located outside of it.

4. Based on the photos of the Milky Way and the understanding that our solar system is located inside, not outside, the galaxy, what might be the shape of the Milky Way?

   A. sphere

   B. disk

   C. cube

5. What evidence did you use to infer a shape for the Milky Way galaxy?

Galileo Galilei used a telescope to distinguish individual stars within the Milky Way.

Explore ONLINE!

The Shape of the Milky Way

In the late 1700s, astronomer William Herschel and his sister Caroline made a map of the Milky Way galaxy. The Herschels estimated distances to different stars using relative brightness. They reasoned that bright stars are closer to Earth and that dim stars are farther from Earth. The Herschels correctly described the Milky Way galaxy as a giant disk with stars and solar systems orbiting its center. Because dim stars appeared to be equally distant from Earth, William Herschel placed our sun at the galaxy's center. William Herschel's placement of our sun was incorrect because huge clouds of dust in space make it difficult to see the most distant stars.

View of a Bicycle Tire from Different Locations

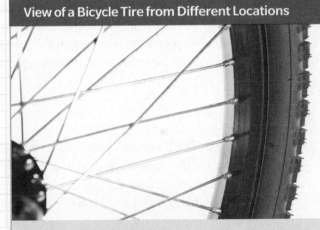

If you look from the center of a bicycle wheel to the rim, the tire appears to be a line extending across your field of view. This is how we see the Milky Way from Earth.

If you look at a spinning tire from a point outside the wheel, more of the tire may be visible. This is how we would view the Milky Way from outside of the galaxy.

Hands-On Lab

Determine Your Location within a Field of Objects

You will record observations of a group of objects from a single location, looking in four different directions. You will analyze a set of similar observations to determine the location of the observer.

Procedure

STEP 1 As a class, crumple about 50 sheets of paper into different-sized balls. Scatter the balls of paper inside a large circle on the floor. The balls should be distributed randomly inside the circle and not in an orderly pattern.

STEP 2 Choose an observation point within the circle (there should be balls in all directions around you). Observe the locations of the balls around you, sitting or bending down so that the balls are as close to eye level as possible.

STEP 3 Look toward the front of the class and make a sketch (on a fresh sheet of paper) of how the balls in your field of view are distributed. Make a note of the direction that you are looking. Then turn 90° and make another sketch. Repeat until you have drawings facing four directions. When finished, you should have four separate sketches, each drawn on a separate sheet of paper.

Analysis

STEP 4 Exchange sketches with a partner. Compare your partner's sketches with the balls in the circle. Based on your partner's sketches, try to determine the point from which your partner's observations were made. Explain how you determined which location the observations were made from.

STEP 5 How could a similar observation method be used to determine where our solar system is located within the Milky Way galaxy?

Earth's Place in the Milky Way

In the early 1900s, Harlow Shapley used telescopes to view large groups of stars called *globular clusters*. All of the globular clusters that Shapley observed were arranged in a large spherical shape. This sphere, composed of many globular clusters, seemed to be centered around a point in space far from Earth. Shapley reasoned that these globular clusters were gathered in a spherical shape because they orbit the gravitational center of the Milky Way galaxy. Shapley could view evidence of the galaxy's center through a telescope, so he concluded that our solar system must lie outside the center. Although the Milky Way is indeed a disk, as the Herschels determined, our sun is not at its center. Shapley's data provided strong evidence that our solar system is located far from the galaxy's center. Over time, scientists used additional observations to determine that our sun lies within one of the outer spiral arms of the Milky Way galaxy.

 EVIDENCE NOTEBOOK

6. How might knowing Earth's position relative to the center of the Milky Way help you make a map of the Milky Way? Record your evidence.

Analyze Dark Portions of Space

When you look at the night sky, there are many dark patches, even in portions of the Milky Way.

7. In addition to globular clusters, which can contain as many as 100,000 stars, Shapley saw areas in space that did not seem to have any stars. Given that telescopes had already been used to find stars in areas of the night sky that previously appeared empty, which of the following statements are most likely to be true? Choose all that apply.

   A. These dark portions contain no stars.

   B. These dark portions contain stars that were too dim for Shapley's telescope to see.

   C. There might be matter such as dust blocking the light from stars.

8. What questions do you have about dark portions of the night sky?

   _____

   _____

   _____

   _____

Analyzing Other Galaxies

Outer space is filled with many different sources of light. In the daytime, sunlight fills the sky and hides most of the other sources of light. At night, however, you can see the moon, hundreds or thousands of stars, and several planets. If you are lucky, you might even see a comet or a streaking meteor.

The round points of light in this photograph are stars. Some of the stars appear to be much brighter than others. The brighter stars may be closer to Earth, or they may simply be hotter and bigger.

9. As you examine the photo, are there any light sources that stand out in comparison to the others? If so, what makes them different?

Unexplained Light Sources

While observing the night sky, many astronomers noticed light sources that looked very different from stars. These objects often appeared larger than stars and, unlike stars, seemed to have fuzzy edges. Some astronomers thought the unknown objects might be clouds of gas inside the Milky Way galaxy. Others thought they might be very large groups of stars, either inside the Milky Way or beyond it. The blurry patch of light that you can see in the photo is one of these light sources, named Andromeda.

Galaxies beyond the Milky Way

In the years following the observation of fuzzy, unexplained light sources, engineers designed larger telescopes for use in research. Large telescopes capture more light than small telescopes. Capturing more light allows the telescope to produce more detailed images of distant objects. This is very similar to the way people can see the details of objects more clearly in bright light than they can in dim light.

In 1919, astronomer Edwin Hubble used the largest telescope in the world to photograph a blurry patch of light known as Andromeda. When Hubble examined the new photographs carefully, he identified faint, individual stars. His discovery led to more questions. How many more stars might be a part of Andromeda? Why were so many stars clustered together? Was Andromeda within the Milky Way galaxy? Hubble would continue to gather data and work collaboratively with other scientists to determine the answers to these questions.

Large telescopes built in the 1900s were much more powerful than earlier telescopes. Edwin Hubble took this photograph of Andromeda using one of these more powerful telescopes.

10. **Language SmArts** What evidence might be needed to determine if a blurry patch of light is located within the Milky Way galaxy or beyond it? Construct a written argument, including claims and reasoning, to present your ideas.

EVIDENCE NOTEBOOK

11. How would the ability to observe other galaxies help in generating models of the Milky Way galaxy? Record your evidence.

Measure Distances Using Brightness

One way to measure the distance to a star is to use the parallax method. Hold your thumb up in front of your face. Close your right eye. Then close your left eye instead. Your thumb will seem to jump when you switch eyes. The closer your thumb is to your face, the bigger the jump will be. Now, imagine that the distance between your eyes is the diameter of Earth's orbit. You can record the position of a star in the sky and then record the position of the star again when Earth is on the other side of its orbit. The star will appear to be in a different place in the sky. This change in the star's position allows astronomers to calculate the star's distance from Earth. This method becomes less accurate the farther stars are from Earth. Astronomers also tried to use the brightness of stars to determine their distance from Earth, but this method had its own problems.

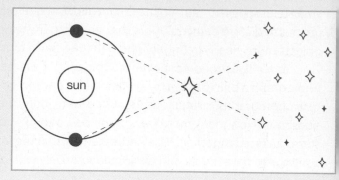

12. Look at the photo of the light bulb. Can you tell how far the light is from the camera? What are some factors that limit your ability to tell how far away objects are?

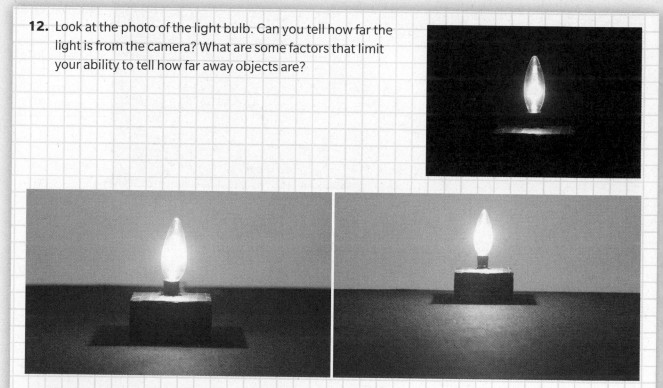

13. The light on the left is about 30 centimeters from the camera. The light on the right is about 100 centimeters from the camera. You can easily tell that these lights are at different distances because of the table. However, imagine that these lights were two stars that seemed equally bright in the night sky. What else would you need to know to determine which light was farther away?

A Universe Full of Galaxies

Edwin Hubble could not use parallax to measure the distance to the dim stars in Andromeda because they were too far away. However, astronomer Henrietta Leavitt had recently discovered Cepheid variable stars. Over regular time intervals, the brightness of a Cepheid variable star changes. Leavitt measured the distances to close Cepheid variable stars. She discovered that the brightest stars took a longer time to change in brightness, while the brightness of the dimmer stars changed more quickly.

Hubble identified several Cepheid variable stars within Andromeda. He observed these stars over time and determined how quickly each star's brightness changed. Then Hubble was able to use his observations and Leavitt's studies to determine how much light these stars were actually producing. Once Hubble knew how much light each star was producing and how bright each star appeared to him, he was able to determine how far away the stars were. He realized that they were very far away! That discovery provided strong evidence that Andromeda is outside the Milky Way and was in fact a galaxy itself.

Cepheid variable stars grow brighter and dimmer over time. This behavior gives astronomers a way to calculate how much light the star is producing.

14. Scientists observe that natural systems display order and consistency. How does this idea relate to Hubble's use of Cepheid variable stars to calculate the distance between Earth and the Andromeda Galaxy?

Explain the Value of Measuring Distances between Objects in Space

15. Recall the example of making a map of a city. How could knowing the distance between you and big buildings or other landmarks in the city help you make a map of your city? Would the same strategies work for larger areas such as a state?

_____

_____

_____

16. How does measuring the distances to stars help you figure out where you are in the universe?

_____

_____

_____

_____

_____

_____

Modeling Scales in the Universe

Since Hubble first found evidence that there were other galaxies, our ability to study the universe has greatly increased. Modern telescopes, including some that observe from outside Earth's atmosphere, provide more detail than Hubble's photographs did. New methods have been developed to measure the distance and speed of objects farther away than Andromeda. Our models of the universe have become more accurate over the last hundred years.

17. After astronomers learned techniques for measuring distances to the planets and the sun, our understanding of the solar system grew. What might be some similar ways in which improved measurements and data collection would affect our view of the universe?

The Whirlpool Galaxy is about 23 million light-years away from the Milky Way. There are many galaxies that are even farther away than this.

The Size of the Milky Way

The Milky Way galaxy is so large that it is almost impossible to imagine its size. To describe the size of galaxies, astronomers needed a new unit of measurement. Astronomers often measure distances in *light-years*. A **light-year** is the distance that light travels in a vacuum in one year. Because light travels about 300,000 kilometers every second, a light-year is a very long distance. A light-year is 9.5×10^{12} km. The Milky Way galaxy measures about 100,000 light-years across. So it would take 100,000 years for light to travel from one side of the Milky Way to the other. That means that light from a star on one side of the galaxy could not be seen on the other side until 100,000 years after the light was produced. And there are galaxies even larger than the Milky Way.

 EVIDENCE NOTEBOOK

18. How does knowing the distance across the Milky Way help to model the galaxy? Record your evidence.

Do the Math
Model the Scale of the Milky Way

The Milky Way galaxy is immense. It is so large that it is hard to describe. Knowing that it measures 100,000 light-years across gives the size a number, but does not really describe the scale. One way to imagine its size is to compare the Milky Way galaxy to our solar system. When numbers of very different sizes are compared, the difference in size can be described using the term *order of magnitude*. If there is a one-order-of-magnitude difference, one measurement is 10 times as large as the other. If there is a two-orders-of-magnitude difference, the larger number is 10 × 10, or 100, times as large.

19. To compare numbers that differ by more than one order of magnitude, it is often easier to use exponents. An exponent tells how many times a number is multiplied by itself. For example, 100 can be represented as 10^2 or as 10 × 10. The number 1,000 can be represented as 10^3 or as 10 × 10 × 10. Each time the exponent is increased, the number is multiplied by itself again.

    _____ can be represented as 10^5 or as 10 × 10 × 10 × 10 × 10.

20. When you read numbers that use exponents, you will notice that a small change in the exponent can indicate a large difference in scale. For example, the thickness of a brick is about 80 millimeters (mm). This number can be written as $8 × 10^1$ mm. The tallest building in the world, the Burj Khalifa, is about 800 meters tall. This height is 800,000, or $8 × 10^5$, mm. How many bricks would there be in a stack of bricks as tall as the Burj Khalifa?

    A. 1,000 (3 orders of magnitude)

    B. 10,000 (4 orders of magnitude)

    C. 100,000 (5 orders of magnitude)

21. The diameter of our solar system is approximately $3 × 10^{10}$ km. The diameter of the Milky Way galaxy is about $9 × 10^{17}$ km. Based on those measurements, the diameter of the galaxy is 30,000,000 times as big as our solar system's which is about _____ orders of magnitude larger.

Stars and Planets in the Milky Way

It is impossible to count all of the stars in the Milky Way. In some areas, there are so many stars that they cannot be seen individually from Earth. Other stars are blocked by clouds of dust. Some stars are not bright enough to see even with our most powerful telescopes. Based on the stars they can observe, astronomers estimate that there are about one hundred billion, or 10^{11}, stars in the Milky Way. If even a small fraction of those stars have planets orbiting them, there would likely be billions of planets in our galaxy.

22. **Write** The number of stars in the Milky Way is enormous. On a separate sheet of paper, write how you would explain this number to another person. Write about comparisons that you could make to other examples of large numbers.

23. This photograph, known as the eXtreme Deep Field (XDF), shows the Hubble Space Telescope's observations of a tiny section of space. The section is so small that it is similar to looking at the sky through a drinking straw. Thousands of galaxies were recorded. What does this tell you about the number of galaxies that exist in the universe?

The XDF photo was made using photographs taken over a period of ten years by the Hubble Space Telescope. It shows a tiny section of the distant universe and contains thousands of galaxies.

Galaxies

Based on data such as the Hubble eXtreme Deep Field photograph, scientists estimate that there are tens of billions of galaxies in the universe. The closest of these galaxies is the Andromeda Galaxy, which is about 3 million light-years from Earth. The most distant galaxies are more than 10 billion light-years away.

The eXtreme Deep Field (XDF) photo shows a portion of the sky that is much smaller than the area taken up by the moon.

Explore Data Collection

24. When astronomers such as Leavitt and Hubble were observing the brightness of stars, they had to manually adjust their telescopes and take images over long periods of time. Modern research telescopes are controlled by computers. What are some ways that being able to control a telescope with a computer might allow us to gather more data about objects in space? Choose all that apply.

A. Computers are able to control the telescopes with more precision than humans.

B. Computers can understand the data better than human observers.

C. Computers can adjust the telescope to take images of an exact location many times.

D. Computers can process data faster than humans.

Continue Your Exploration

Name: _____   **Date:** _____

Check out the path below or go online to choose one of the other paths shown.

The Kepler Mission

- **Hands-On Labs**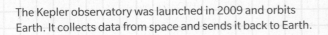
- **Other Galaxies**
- **Propose Your Own Path**

Go online to choose one of these other paths.

The Kepler Mission is NASA's first exploratory data collection mission that is specifically designed to find Earth-sized planets. From an observation point above Earth's atmosphere, the Kepler observatory measures the light coming from distant stars. As it constantly observes more than 100,000 stars for years at a time, the Kepler instruments can detect small changes in a star's brightness. These changes can indicate that a planet is orbiting the star.

1. Astronomers use the Kepler observatory to search the areas around stars for planets that are similar to Earth. As a planet passes in front of its star, the brightness of the starlight reaching the telescope changes. How might the change in the brightness of a star give information about how large a planet is?

The Kepler observatory was launched in 2009 and orbits Earth. It collects data from space and sends it back to Earth.

Continue Your Exploration

2. Which statements describe limitations that could affect the ability of the Kepler observatory to measure the size of a planet? Circle all that apply.

   A. Only planets that move in front of a star can be measured by this method.

   B. Different stars are located at different distances from Earth.

   C. Stars do not all have the same diameter.

   D. Some stars' brightness can vary over time.

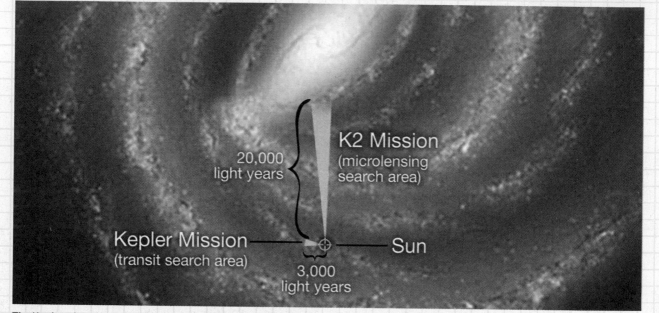

The Kepler observatory was originally used to search for planets that were less than 3,000 light-years from Earth. Under the K2 mission, it was used to search for planets up to 20,000 light-years away.

3. The Kepler observatory only observes a tiny portion of the night sky, as shown in the image. Even so, it has detected thousands of planets. What does this tell you about the number of planets in the Milky Way galaxy?

4. **Collaborate** Research and summarize some of the recent discoveries that have been made using the Kepler observatory. Research and define what the habitable zone is. Explain how the habitable zone relates to the Kepler observatory's mission.

Can You Explain It?

Name: _____   Date: _____

How can we make a model of the Milky Way galaxy that shows Earth's location?

 EVIDENCE NOTEBOOK

Refer to the notes in your Evidence Notebook to help you construct an explanation for how scientists model Earth within the Milky Way galaxy.

1. State your argument. Make sure your claims fully explain how Earth's location in relation to the rest of the Milky Way can be determined.

2. Summarize the evidence you have gathered to support your claims and explain your reasoning.

Checkpoints

Answer the following questions to check your understanding of the lesson.

Use the photo to answer Question 3.

3. If an observer looked out from a planet near the center of this galaxy, what would it look like to that observer?

   A. a broad band of stars forming a ring around the planet

   B. a sphere of stars evenly spread in every direction

   C. a spiral shape with arms reaching out from a center

   D. a band of stars in one direction, with fewer stars in other directions

4. We can measure the brightness of a star in a galaxy to tell how far away that galaxy is. Which assumptions are necessary when using this method? Select all that apply.

   A. Galaxies contain very bright stars.

   B. We can determine the amount of light a star produces.

   C. Stars in the galaxy are similar to stars in the Milky Way.

   D. The star does not have any large planets.

Use the photo to answer Question 5.

5. Most of the points of light in the photo are likely stars / galaxies. The larger bright object toward the center of the photo could possibly be a galaxy / universe because of its fuzzier edges. To definitively tell what this object is, you would need to identify stars inside the light and measure how bright / far away those stars are.

6. Two stars on opposite sides of the night sky appear very different. One star is very bright and can be seen before the sky is completely dark. The other can barely be seen on a dark night. Which of the following could be a reason that these two stars have different apparent brightnesses? Select all that apply.

   A. The brighter star emits much more light than the dimmer star..

   B. A planet orbiting the dimmer star blocks most of its light.

   C. The brighter star is much closer to Earth than the dimmer star.

   D. Clouds of dust block some of the light from the dimmer star.

Interactive Review

Complete this section to review the main concepts of the lesson.

The Milky Way galaxy is a large group of stars that includes our sun.

A. Explain how evidence pointed toward our current understanding of the Milky Way's shape.

There are many other galaxies beyond the Milky Way.

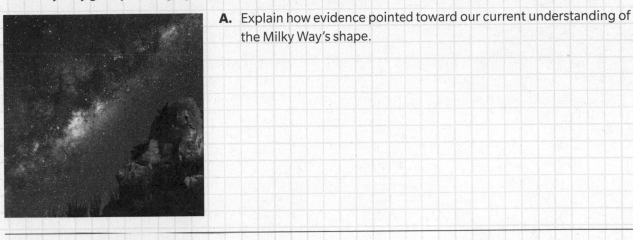

B. How can it be shown that galaxies other than the Milky Way exist?

Our sun is one of many billions of stars in the Milky Way, which is one of many billions of galaxies in the universe.

C. Explain why using measurements such as the light-year becomes necessary when discussing distances in the universe.

Gravity in the Universe

These two spiral galaxies in space move toward each other.

By the end of this lesson . . .

you will be able to explain the role of gravity in the universe.

Go online to view the digital version of
the Hands-On Lab for this lesson and to
download additional lab resources.

CAN YOU EXPLAIN IT?

What could explain the motion of these stars?

This image shows the paths of stars near the center of the Milky Way galaxy as observed from Earth over several years.

Explore ONLINE!

1. Look at the path of one of the stars. How does the star appear to move?

2. Compare the paths of all the stars. How are the paths of the stars similar, and how are they different?

 EVIDENCE NOTEBOOK As you explore the lesson, gather evidence to help explain the movement of stars.

Applying Newton's Laws of Motion

Newton's Laws of Motion

When you throw a ball of crumpled paper, how do you know which way it will go? Objects move in predictable ways. In the late 1600s, Sir Isaac Newton published a set of physical laws describing how things move when acted on by forces. These laws are known as Newton's laws of motion. The three laws of motion can be used to describe how forces acting on an object affect the motion of the object.

Since Newton's time, other scientists have discovered that objects that move at extreme speeds or those that have extremely small or large masses move in ways not described exactly by these laws. But Newton's laws of motion have proven to be very useful for describing and predicting the motion of objects moving at speeds we encounter in our everyday lives. These laws have helped humans to predict the motions of objects on Earth and in space.

Newton's Laws of Motion	
First Law	Unless acted on by an unbalanced force, an object in motion tends to stay in motion and an object at rest tends to stay at rest
Second Law	When an unbalanced force acts on an object, the object accelerates. The net force is equal to the mass of the object multiplied by its acceleration.
Third Law	When one object exerts a force on another object, the second object exerts an equal force on the first object in the opposite direction.

3. **Discuss** With a partner, discuss Newton's laws of motion and give an example of each from your everyday life.

4. Consider the motion of a passenger on the swing ride. Use Newton's laws of motion to explain the person's motion during the ride.

Forces affect the path of each passenger on this swing ride.

Explore ONLINE!

Gravity and Apparent Weight

Have you ever noticed how you sometimes feel heavier or lighter in an elevator? This happens because the forces acting on your body change when the elevator accelerates. Imagine a person standing in an elevator that is not moving. Note that motion is measured relative to a reference point. In this case, the reference point is the ground. Newton's laws tell us that the force of gravity pulling the person down is balanced by an upward force from the elevator floor. **Gravity** is a force of attraction between objects due to their masses. The upward force is what the person feels and calls weight.

Now imagine that the elevator begins to accelerate upward. The person also accelerates upward. We know from Newton's second law that an unbalanced force causes the acceleration. In this case, the upward force on the person is greater than the downward force of gravity, and the person feels heavier. Their apparent weight is greater than their weight due to gravity alone. When the elevator reaches a constant speed, the forces are balanced again and the person feels their normal weight.

5. A person is standing in an elevator on Earth. What type of motion must the elevator have for the person's apparent weight to be 0 N? Use Newton's laws of motion to support your claim.

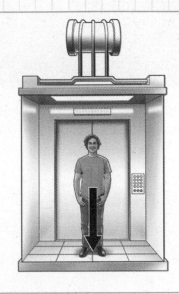

The arrow shows the force of gravity acting on the person. The elevator exerts an upward force (not shown) on the person. This upward force may vary.

Artificial Gravity

When you see a video made on the International Space Station, the astronauts appear to float around freely. In these videos, the frame of reference is the space station itself. We are comparing the positions of the astronauts and objects to the space station. Sometimes people say these astronauts orbiting Earth are in "zero gravity," but the pull of Earth's gravity is acting on the space station and its contents. The space station and its contents are all essentially "falling" at a constant rate around the Earth. Because everything is falling, there is nothing to apply the reaction force that causes the sensation of weight. The apparent weight of the astronauts is 0 N; they feel weightless.

Other areas of space are far from any strong gravitational fields. Astronauts in these areas would experience low gravity. "Weightless" environments can lead to health problems, including loss of bone mass. If people were ever to travel to other star systems, they would have to spend long periods without the effects of gravity. If such space travel were to occur, a system of "artificial gravity" would be very useful.

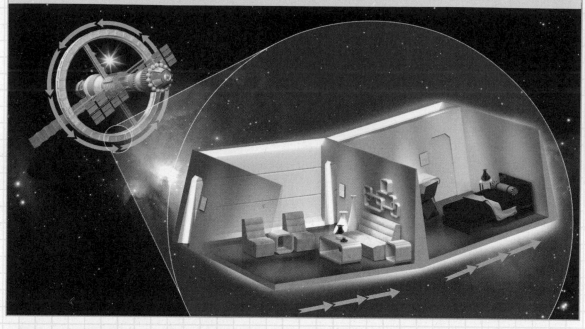

Long-Distance Space Travel Ship

This rotating ship could provide a force that feels similar to how gravity affects people on Earth.

6. Engineer It | Analyze an Artificial Gravity System The diagram shows a proposed design for a ship that could be used for long-distance space travel. Explain why the ship must rotate so that passengers feel effects similar to gravity.

Apply Newton's Laws to Circular Motion

7. An object is moving in a circular path at a constant speed. Based on Newton's laws of motion, which of these statements must be true? Select all that apply.

   A. The velocity is constant because the speed is constant, so there are no forces acting on the object.

   B. The speed is constant, so there are no forces acting on the object.

   C. The velocity is not constant because the direction is not constant, so there is an unbalanced force acting on the object.

   D. The speed is constant, so the forces acting on the object are balanced.

Modeling Gravity

It is the nature of science to build on previous discoveries. Tycho Brahe was an astronomer who made detailed observations of the motions of the planets, in particular the motion of Mars. After his death, his student Johannes Kepler analyzed Brahe's observations. Kepler wrote three mathematical laws, based on Brahe's data, that described the motions of the planets. While Kepler's laws could be used to predict the motions of the planets, they did not explain why the planets moved the way they did. Newton was able to use Kepler's laws to help develop a model of gravity that explained the motions of the planets and other bodies in the solar system.

Tycho Brahe 1546–1601   Johannes Kepler 1571–1630   Sir Issac Newton 1643–1727

8. Newton said, "If I have seen further than others, it is by standing upon the shoulders of giants." Explain the meaning of this quotation.

The Law of Universal Gravitation

Sir Isaac Newton believed that the same force that causes objects to fall to the ground also causes the motion of the planets. That force is gravity. In 1687, Newton published his work including the law of universal gravitation.

The law of universal gravitation states that all matter attracts all other matter. There is an attractive force of gravity between any two objects. This force is proportional to the mass of each object, and it is inversely proportional to the square of the distance between the centers of the objects. Mathematically, the law can written as

$$F = G\left(\frac{m_1 \times m_2}{d^2}\right)$$

In this equation, F represents the force of gravity, m_1 and m_2 represent the masses of the two objects, and d represents the distance between the objects. G is the gravitational constant, and its value depends on the units of mass and distance. The value of the gravitational constant was first measured many years after Newton published his work.

9. **Do the Math** Which of the following changes will increase the force of gravity between two masses? Use the formula $F = G\left(\frac{m_1 \times m_2}{d^2}\right)$.

A. m_1 increases

B. m_1 decreases

C. m_2 increases

D. m_2 decreases

E. d increases

F. d decreases

The Cavendish Experiment

Almost 100 years after Newton published the law of universal gravitation, Henry Cavendish performed an investigation that we now know as the Cavendish experiment. This is the first known experiment to measure the force of gravity between objects.

The setup, shown below, begins with two small masses hanging from a frame. This frame was supported by a wire so it could rotate. Since even a small breeze would rotate the frame, Cavendish enclosed the entire setup in a shed. Inside the shed, two large lead balls hung on another support. When the large lead balls moved near the smaller masses, the smaller masses were attracted to the larger masses, causing the frame to rotate. By carefully measuring the rotation of the frame, Cavendish could calculate the force of gravity between the small and large masses.

After this experiment, scientists were able to use Cavendish's measurements and the law of universal gravitation to calculate the gravitational constant and the masses of Earth and other celestial bodies.

10. **Discuss** With a partner, discuss the design of this experiment. How do you think this experiment could be improved?

Cavendish Experimental Setup

A frame supporting small masses rotates as the smaller masses are attracted by gravity toward the larger masses. Cavendish used telescopes to observe the rotation of the frame in his shed, so that his own mass would be farther away from the apparatus. If he stood next to the apparatus, his own mass might have interfered with the movement he was trying to observe.

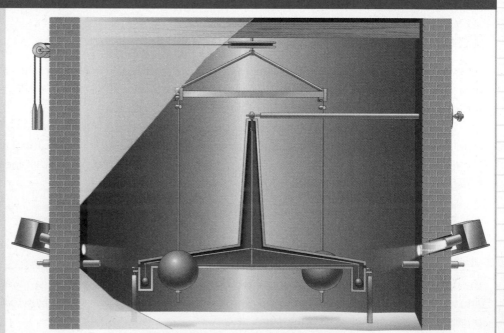

11. The art shows the masses in Cavendish's apparatus from above. In position A, the forces on the smaller masses are balanced. Draw how you expect the orientation of the rod and smaller masses to change when the larger masses are moved to position B.

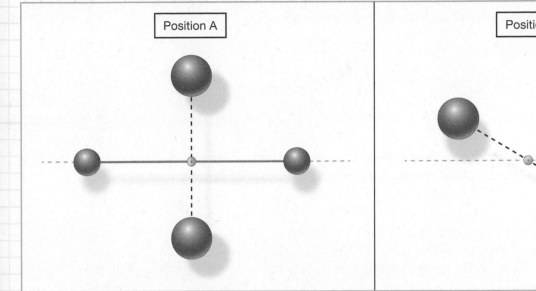

Position A

Position B

Gravity Shapes Celestial Bodies

Think about the shape of the Earth, moon, sun, and other planets. What do they have in common? These bodies and other large celestial bodies all appear to be spherical in shape. Is this just a coincidence? No; gravity has a role in shaping massive celestial bodies. As the mass of an object increases, so does its gravitational field. This gravitational field pulls in all directions with the same strength. Think about what would happen to a lump of clay if you were to press on it equally in all directions at the same time. How would the shape of the clay change?

While gravity is the primary reason objects are spherical, other factors may cause an object to not be exactly spherical. An object's rotation, or the material the object is made of, may cause deviations in shape. Also, less massive objects do not have enough gravity to affect the shape of the object.

This bubble is spherical in shape because the air pressure that shapes the bubble acts evenly in all directions.

12. How does the way that air pressure shapes the bubble relate to the way that gravity shapes massive celestial bodies?

13. **Do the Math | Compare the Gravity of Different Planets** Remember that the gravitational force between two objects depends on the masses of both objects and the distance between them. Imagine a planet that has the same radius as Earth but only half its mass. How would the gravitational force between you and this planet compare to the gravitational force between you and Earth if you stood on the surface of each planet? Explain your answer.

14. **Write** Write a short story or perform a one-act play demonstrating how life would be different on a planet with half the gravitational force of Earth at its surface.

Explain Earth's Shape

We know from satellite data that Earth is not exactly a sphere. Earth bulges out near the equator and is slightly flattened near the poles. Newton's first law says that an object in motion will stay in motion, so the points on the surface of a spinning object have a tendency to continue moving at the same speed in the same direction.

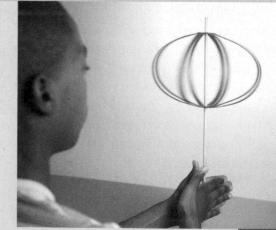

Notice how this sphere of paper deforms when it spins.

Explore ONLINE!

15. How does the model shown in the photo relate to the shape of Earth? Select all that apply.

   A. The model shows that a spherical object may deform when it spins.

   B. Places near the equator have a greater tendency to move outward due to their velocity than places near the poles.

   C. The paper sphere is hollow, so this model does not relate to the shape of Earth.

   D. The faster an object spins, the more likely it is to deform.

Exploring Gravity's Role in Orbital Motion

Projectile Motion

An object that is launched or thrown is called a *projectile*. Once a projectile is launched, its motion is controlled by the force of gravity. When you throw an object into the air, it goes up for a while and then falls. The gravitational pull between the object and Earth causes it to fall back toward Earth's center. Projectiles may also encounter some air resistance, but their acceleration is mostly due to gravity. An airplane would not be considered a projectile because its motion is not primarily controlled by gravity.

Explore ONLINE!

The basketball is a projectile. Notice the path of the ball as it travels toward the hoop.

16. Use Newton's laws of motion and the law of universal gravitation to explain the motion of the basketball during a free-throw attempt.

The Effect of Velocity on Projectile Motion

Think about how a ball moves when you throw it in the air. Does it make a difference whether you toss it straight up or at an angle? What about if you throw it faster or slower? The velocity, or speed and direction, of the launch determines what path a projectile follows. When analyzing the expected path of a projectile, it is important to notice in which direction the object will accelerate due to gravity. If acceleration is in the same direction as the velocity of an object, the speed of the object will increase, but its direction will not change. If acceleration is in the opposite direction, its speed will decrease, but the direction will not change. If the acceleration of an object is perpendicular to its velocity, the speed will not change, but the direction will. Acceleration in another direction will cause a change in speed and direction.

Hands-On Lab
Explore the Motion of a Falling Object

You will explore how the velocity of a ball rolling on a table affects its path after it rolls off the table and becomes a projectile.

MATERIALS
- colored pencils
- paper
- steel balls or marbles
- table

Procedure

STEP 1 Based on your knowledge of projectiles and previous observations of motion, predict the path of a ball after it very slowly rolls off the edge of a table. Draw your predicted path on the image below using a red colored pencil.

STEP 2 Roll a ball very slowly off the edge of the table. Carefully observe the path that the ball follows as it falls. In the same drawing area as your prediction, draw the actual path that you observed, using a blue colored pencil.

STEP 3 Make a prediction of the path of a ball after it rolls a little more quickly, but still fairly slowly, off the edge of a table. Draw your predicted path below in red.

STEP 4 Roll a ball slowly off the edge of a table. Draw the actual path in blue in the same area as your prediction.

STEP 5 Make a prediction of the path of a ball after it rolls more quickly off the edge of a table. Draw your predicted path in red.

STEP 6 Roll a ball more quickly off the edge of a table. Draw the actual path in blue in the same area as your prediction.

Analysis

STEP 7 How did the results of each step affect your predictions for future steps?

STEP 8 How does the horizontal velocity of the ball on the table affect the path of the ball when it falls off the table?

17. If the cannonball in the image were launched a fifth time at a much faster velocity, what would happen to the motion of the ball?

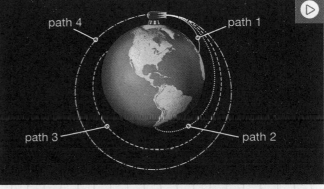

This image shows a thought experiment in which a cannonball is launched at increasing velocities. Path 1 is the slowest and path 4 is the fastest.

Velocity and Orbits

A *satellite* is an object that orbits a more massive object. An **orbit** is the path that a particular object follows as it travels around another body in space. A natural satellite forms naturally in space and is attracted by gravity toward a more massive object. Gravity holds the satellite in orbit. The moon is a natural satellite of Earth. Earth is also orbited by about 2,300 human-made satellites and countless bits of debris. These satellites include space telescopes and satellites that provide communications, weather observations, and navigation signals.

Satellites do not all orbit at the same distance from Earth. Some satellites travel in a low Earth orbit (LEO) between 160 km and 2,000 km above sea level. Some satellites travel in a high Earth orbit (HEO) more than about 35,786 km above sea level. The distance between an orbiting satellite and the object it orbits is related to the satellite's speed. An object in LEO must travel faster than an object in HEO. An object in LEO will also experience air drag from the atmosphere. Without additional thrust to maintain its speed, the object will slow down, and gravity will pull it back to Earth's surface.

18. Language SmArts In a *geostationary orbit,* the satellite remains directly above a specific location on Earth at all times. A satellite in geostationary orbit will complete an orbit every 24 hours. This is very useful for communication and navigation satellites. Geostationary satellites must orbit at a specific height above sea level. Which evidence from the text helps to support this claim?

Not all orbits are circular; in fact, most are elliptical. To see why this happens, we must analyze the velocity of the orbiting object and the object's acceleration due to gravity at each point along its path. Remember that an object accelerates in the direction of an unbalanced force on the object. A greater force causes a greater acceleration, and the force of gravity between two objects is greater when the objects are closer together.

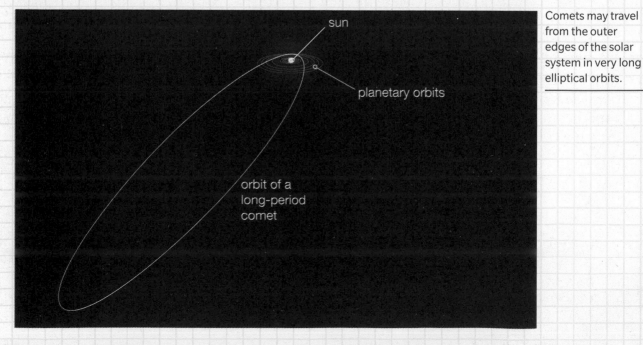

sun

planetary orbits

orbit of a long-period comet

Comets may travel from the outer edges of the solar system in very long elliptical orbits.

19. At each position of the comet shown, draw an arrow representing the strength and direction of the force of gravity on the comet.

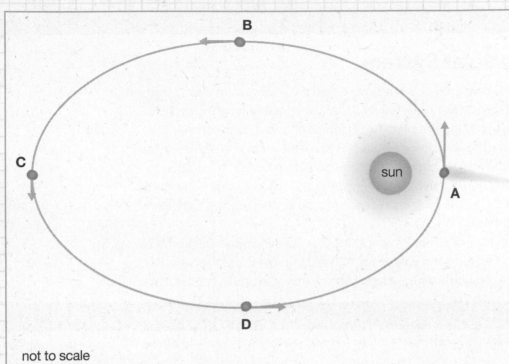

The blue arrows show the comet's velocity at different points in its orbital path.

not to scale

20 **Discuss** With a partner, discuss how the gravitational force between the sun and comet changes the velocity, or speed and direction, of the comet at each position along its orbit.

 EVIDENCE NOTEBOOK

21. What causes an object to orbit another object? Record your evidence.

 Engineer It
Choose a Launch Site

22. An object must move very quickly in order to reach orbit. Think about how Earth itself spins. Where is the best place to locate a launch site to get an object into orbit? Explain your answer.

_____

_____

_____

_____

_____

_____

Explaining the Motions of Objects in Space

Matter in the Solar System

Billions of years ago, the matter that currently makes up the solar system was spread out across a vast region of space. Over time, gravitational attractions among the particles of matter caused them to pull together into large clumps of matter. One of these clumps became our sun. The sun contains about 99.8% of the mass in our solar system. Other clumps formed the planets, comets, asteroids and other bodies. In addition to contributing to the formation of these bodies, gravity is also the force that holds these bodies in orbit around the sun. Gravity also keeps the solar system moving together with other star systems in the Milky Way galaxy.

This same process has occurred across the universe, forming other star systems and galaxies. These star systems and galaxies are all held together by gravity. Just like planets in a star system orbiting a central mass, galaxies may also orbit a central mass.

The Solar System

Most of the mass of the solar system is found in the sun. Most of the volume between the planets is empty space.

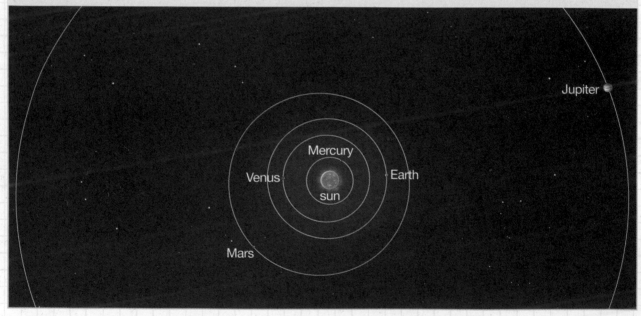

23. Why do the planets and other bodies in the solar system orbit the sun rather than another body in the solar system?

Motion within the Solar System

When the solar system formed, matter was moving in many different directions. Particles near each other were drawn together by gravity and formed new, larger masses. The velocity of each new mass depended on the masses and velocities of the particles that collided to form each new mass. Over time, gravity continued to pull masses together, forming larger and larger masses. These larger masses continued moving through space. As these larger masses moved through space, the force of gravity continued to act on them, causing some of them to orbit other, larger masses. Without the force of gravity, masses near each other would continue to move in straight lines, unless they collided with other objects.

24. How does gravity influence the motion of objects in the solar system?

Motion beyond the Solar System

It is easy to see how gravity works in our daily lives. Gravity also can be used to model the motion of planets and other objects beyond the solar system. Observations made using large telescopes and other instruments have shown that gravity appears to act on objects throughout the universe. For example, we have seen comets move past the outer planets of the solar system and return, so we know that gravity continues to have an effect outside of the solar system.

When we look at the shapes of galaxies and nebulas, we see evidence of circular or elliptical paths of stars, planets, and star systems. Gravity is the force that shapes these paths. We have observed stars and galaxies near each other moving toward one another in ways that strongly suggest the force of gravity is pulling the bodies toward each other.

Galaxies have a variety of sizes and shapes.

25. How might the structure of the universe be different if gravity were not acting throughout the universe? What would you observe?

Gravitational Fields of Massive Objects

The planet Earth has about 10^{23} times more mass than a human (that is a one followed by 23 zeros). The sun is 333,000 times the mass of Earth. There are uncountable stars that are more massive than our sun. There are other objects even more massive than those large stars: black holes. Black holes have masses much larger than that of the sun, but their diameters can be as small as a few kilometers. As a result, the force of gravity at their surface is extremely strong. Even light is not able to escape the gravitational force of these objects, which is why they are called black holes.

Recall that the force of gravity between two objects is proportional to the mass of the two objects and inversely proportional to the square of the distance between them. Because a black hole is so massive, it has the potential to affect the motion of many objects around it, even at a large distance.

26. Imagine two planets of equal mass. Planet A orbits the sun, while Planet B orbits a black hole that is 10,000 times the mass of the sun. The distances from each planet to the bodies they orbit are equal. How does the gravitational force between Planet A and the sun compare with the force between Planet B and the black hole?

EVIDENCE NOTEBOOK

27. Since we cannot see a black hole, what evidence could be used to locate a black hole? Record your evidence

Show Evidence of Gravity in the Universe

From a distance, this galaxy looks like a single object, but it is really made up billions of stars, planets, and other bodies, all orbiting a central point.

28. What evidence in the photo indicates that gravity works throughout the universe in the same way that it works in the solar system?

_____

_____

_____

Continue Your Exploration

Name: _____ **Date:** _____

Check out the path below or go online to choose one of the other paths shown.

Building a Space Elevator

- **Hands-On Labs** ✋
- **The Expanding Universe**
- **Propose Your Own Path**

Go online to choose one of these other paths.

Getting into space with rockets is expensive and potentially dangerous. To get to the top of a tall building, you simply take an elevator. Someday we may be able to build an elevator to space, but the technology is not available yet.

An elevator to space would be many times longer than the tallest buildings on Earth. Tall buildings are very massive and require strong materials to keep them from collapsing due to their weight. The materials for a space elevator would have to be very light but strong. Scientists are researching materials that would be strong enough yet light enough for a space elevator.

Another challenge is how to build the space elevator. Even with very lightweight materials, a cable long enough would be very massive and difficult to support. If we started building from space, we could use gravity to pull the cable down to Earth. The cable would run from a platform in geostationary orbit to a place on Earth. To help keep this system in orbit, we could attach a massive counterweight to the outer end of the cable. This mass would keep the elevator cable tight, in the same way that swinging a mass on a string keeps the string tight.

Building a space elevator would be a large and expensive task. Once built, however, the elevator could be a cost-effective and safe way to get people and objects into space and back.

The Petronas Towers in Kuala Lumpur, Malaysia reach a height of 452 meters from the ground.

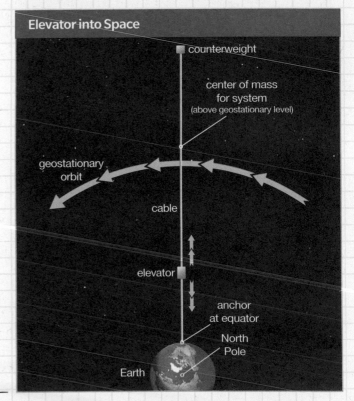

Elevator into Space

counterweight

center of mass for system
(above geostationary level)

geostationary orbit

cable

elevator

anchor at equator

North Pole

Earth

The cable would act as an elevator shaft, guiding a load from the surface to a platform near the system's center of mass.

Continue Your Exploration

1. The Petronas Towers reach 452 m up from the ground. A space elevator cable would need to be around 100,000 km long. How many times longer is the space elevator cable than the height of the Petronas Towers, to the nearest whole number?

2 How would a space elevator make it easier to put people or objects into space?

3. Why does the space elevator need a counterweight?

4. What type of background knowledge would someone need to have in order to successfully build the space elevator?

5. **Collaborate** Work with a small group to consider things that might interfere with the building of a space elevator. Make a presentation about the expected problems and how you could address those problems.

Can You Explain It?

Name: _____   **Date:** _____

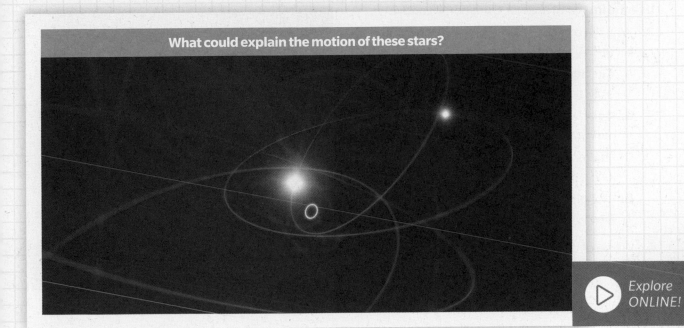

What could explain the motion of these stars?

 Explore ONLINE!

 EVIDENCE NOTEBOOK

Refer to the notes in your Evidence Notebook to help you construct an explanation for the motion of stars in our galaxy.

1. State your claim. Make sure your claim fully explains the motion of these stars near the center of the Milky Way galaxy.

2. Summarize the evidence you have gathered to support your claim and explain your reasoning.

Checkpoints

Answer the following questions to check your understanding of the lesson.

Use the image to answer Questions 3 and 4.

3. Why did the route of Voyager 2 change, without firing its thrusters, as it passed Jupiter?

   A. Gravitational force between Jupiter and Voyager 2 pulled it into a new route.

   B. Solar winds pushed Voyager 2 into a new path.

   C. Jupiter blocked the sun's gravitational pull on Voyager 2.

   D. The gravity of Jupiter caused Voyager 2 to become its satellite.

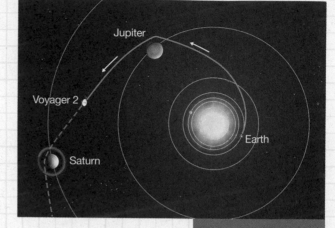

4. Which of the following did scientists and engineers need to know to plan Voyager 2's path through the solar system? Choose all that apply.

   A. the positions of the planets

   B. the masses of the planets

   C. the mass of Voyager 2

   D. Newton's laws of motion and the law of universal gravitation

Explore ONLINE!

Use the graph to answer Question 5.

5. The chihuahua is in an elevator. What is the elevator doing at 22 seconds?

   A. It is moving up at a constant velocity.

   B. It is moving down at a constant velocity.

   C. It is accelerating upward.

   D. It is accelerating downward.

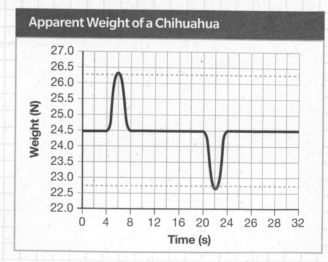

Apparent Weight of a Chihuahua

---

6. The law of universal gravitation is a(n) model / experiment of gravity. The law of universal gravitation can be used with / without Newton's laws of motion to explain the motions of bodies in space.

7. Tides occur because of the gravitational pull of three bodies on Earth's surface: the sun, the moon, and Earth itself. Order these objects by strength of their pull on the oceans, from greatest to smallest.

   A. Earth, moon, sun

   B. moon, Earth, sun

   C. sun, Earth, moon

Interactive Review

Complete this section to review the main concepts of the lesson.

The motion of objects on Earth and in space can be explained by Newton's laws of motion.

A. What is necessary to cause the motion of an object to change?

Newton's law of universal gravitation combined with Newton's laws of motion gave scientists tools to predict the motion of objects in space and on Earth.

B. Why is it useful to model gravity?

Orbits in the solar system range from near-perfect circles to very elongated ellipses.

C. How does the speed of an object in an elliptical orbit around the sun change as the object moves around the sun?

The force of gravity in the universe is responsible for the formation of various celestial bodies and for their motion.

D. How do the structures of galaxies give evidence of gravity?

Choose one of the activities to explore how this unit connects to other topics.

☐ Physical Science Connection

Structure of Other Solar Systems Until recently, astronomers expected that other planetary systems would be similar to our solar system. They expected to find small, rocky inner planets and large, gas giant planets farther from the center. However, some distant planetary systems that have been recently discovered include such anomalies as "Super-Jupiters" close to the central sun.

Research current hypotheses about how extrasolar planetary systems form. Describe how these systems inform our understanding of our own solar system and galaxy. Make a multimedia presentation to share what you learned with your class.

☐ Technology Connection

Satellite Studies of Archaeological Sites A 15-year-old Canadian boy did a science fair project in which he compared constellation charts with the locations of Mayan cultural sites. He tested his hypothesis about a "missing" site by using satellite images that show what appear to be the remains of pyramids in Mexico's Yucatan Peninsula. This example shows how space-based technology can be used to study Earth as well as distant stars.

Research how satellite technology is being used in the study of archaeology and human history. Choose an archaeological site or historical event, and prepare a report about how satellite images improved scientific understanding of the site or event.

☐ Social Studies Connection

Navigating with Polaris The star Polaris is also called the North Star. It can be located as the last star in the "handle" of the Little Dipper constellation. In the Northern Hemisphere, Polaris is visible year-round in the night sky. Because its position in the sky is predictable, many cultures used Polaris as a reference point for navigating.

Research the significance of Polaris in navigation. Prepare a skit to perform for your class that explains how a culture or group of people used Polaris to find their way when traveling.

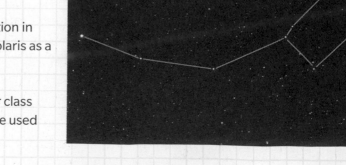

Name: _____ Date: _____

Complete this review to check your understanding of the unit.

Use the diagram to answer Questions 1–3.

1. Compare the internal structures of the terrestrial planets. How do the scales of the internal layers of the planets compare? Select all that apply.

   A. Mars and Venus have thick crusts compared to Earth and Mercury.

   B. Earth and Venus are the most similar to each other in terms of internal structure.

   C. Mars has the largest iron core of the four.

   D. Mercury and Mars have larger silicate mantles than Venus and Earth do.

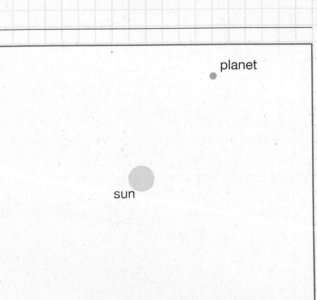

Structure of the Terrestrial Planets

Earth Venus

Mercury Mars

- Silicate crust
- Silicate mantle
- Liquid iron core
- Solid iron core

Credit: Adapted figure from Astronomy Notes. Copyright © Nick Strobel. Reprinted courtesy of Nick Strobel.

2. Compare the diameters of the terrestrial planets. How do the relative sizes of the planets compare? Select all that apply.

   A. Mars is about the size of Earth's liquid and solid iron core.

   B. Mercury is larger then Venus's liquid and solid iron core.

   C. Mercury is about the size of Mars's iron core.

   D. Venus could fit inside Earth's silicate crust.

3. When these terrestrial planets formed, more dense / less dense materials sank to the center and more dense / less dense materials stayed near the surface. Within the solar system, a similar / different pattern occurred. The inner, terrestrial planets are more dense / less dense, and the outer, gas giant planets are more dense / less dense.

Use the diagram to answer Question 4.

4. The image shows the location of one planet and the sun. Draw arrows and ellipses on the diagram to show:

   • the direction of the planet through space if it were not affected by the sun's gravity

   • the direction of the sun's gravitational effect on the planet

   • the shape and direction of the resulting orbit

planet

sun

5. Complete the table by providing at least one example of how these space topics relate to each big concept.

Topic	Systems and Models	Scale	Structure
Earth	Earth contains many systems. Earth is also part of the Earth-sun-moon system, the solar system, the galaxy, and the universe.		
Solar System			
Gravity			
Orbit			

Name: _____ Date: _____

Use the image to answer Questions 6–9.

6. How can this set of nesting toys be used as a model of the systems that make up the universe?

7. If you were asked to label each doll as a part of the universe, which doll would represent the following: the solar system, the universe, Earth, the Milky Way galaxy, and the Earth-sun-moon system?

8. Is this model to scale? Explain your answer by using evidence from the unit and scientific reasoning.

9. Identify at least three limitations of this model of the universe. How could you modify this model to improve it?

Use the images to answer Questions 10–13.

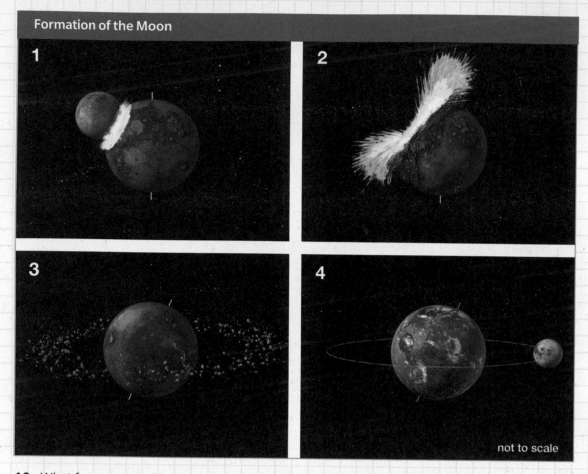

Formation of the Moon

not to scale

10. What forces were acting on Earth and on the impacting object before they collided?

11. What role did gravity play in the formation of the moon?

12. How is the formation of the moon around Earth similar to the formation of Earth around the sun? How is it different?

13. Why does the moon orbit Earth in the same direction that Earth orbits the sun?

Name: _____

Date: _____

What role does gravity play in a lunar landing?

An understanding of gravity has played an important role in the space program and in the lunar landings. You have been invited to participate in the Constellation Program, which aims to have another lunar landing and "sustained human presence" in space in the future. Learn about the space program and how they rely on an understanding of gravity to plan missions and outposts in space. You will focus on how gravity affects sending people and materials into space and landing people and materials safely on other bodies. You will also learn about how changes in gravity affect the human body.

Constellation Mission Diagram

This diagram shows the proposed Constellation mission to land on the moon and includes the outbound and inbound trajectories and landing areas.

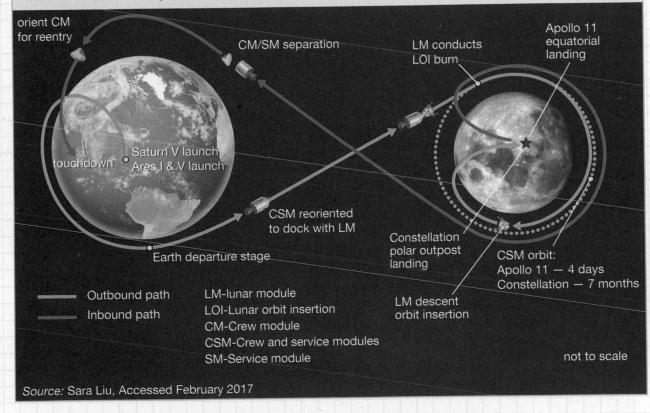

orient CM for reentry

CM/SM separation

LM conducts LOI burn

Apollo 11 equatorial landing

touchdown

Saturn V launch
Ares I & V launch

CSM reoriented to dock with LM

Earth departure stage

Constellation polar outpost landing

CSM orbit:
Apollo 11 — 4 days
Constellation — 7 months

LM descent orbit insertion

Outbound path
Inbound path

LM-lunar module
LOI-Lunar orbit insertion
CM-Crew module
CSM-Crew and service modules
SM-Service module

not to scale

Source: Sara Liu, Accessed February 2017

The steps below will help guide your research and help you write a proposal.

1. **Ask a Question** Develop questions you will need to answer to write a proposal for sending a manned spacecraft to the moon to develop a colony. Think about how gravity plays a role in what items are brought into space, how people and the spaceships move around, and the structure of the spaceship.

2. **Conduct Research** Research answers to the relevant questions using NASA and the Constellation Program as resources. Think about answers to how gravity affects people's bodies, supplies for travel, and spacecraft movement.

3. **Evaluate Data** Analyze your research to identify important variables that you need to consider in your proposal. Include a list of ways that you will address gravity in your plan.

4. **Write a Proposal** Based on your research, construct a written proposal for sending a manned spacecraft to the moon to develop a colony.

5. **Communicate** Present your recommendation about a lunar colony to the class.

 **Self-Check**

	I identified and accounted for the role gravity plays in sending people into space and landing them back on Earth or another body in space.
	I researched the Constellation Program and how the space program relies on an understanding of gravity in space.
	I constructed a written proposal for sending a manned spacecraft to the moon to develop a colony.
	My proposal and recommendation were clearly communicated to others.

Glossary

Pronunciation Key							
Sound	Symbol	Example	Respelling	Sound	Symbol	Example	Respelling
ă	a	pat	PAT	ŏ	ah	bottle	BAHT'l
ā	ay	pay	PAY	ō	oh	toe	TOH
âr	air	care	KAIR	ô	aw	caught	KAWT
ä	ah	father	FAH•ther	ôr	ohr	roar	ROHR
är	ar	argue	AR•gyoo	oi	oy	noisy	NOYZ•ee
ch	ch	chase	CHAYS	o͞o	u	book	BUK
ě	e	pet	PET	o͞o	oo	boot	BOOT
ě (at end of a syllable)	eh	settee lessee	seh•TEE leh•SEE	ou	ow	pound	POWND
ěr	ehr	merry	MEHR•ee	s	s	center	SEN•ter
ē	ee	beach	BEECH	sh	sh	cache	CASH
g	g	gas	GAS	ŭ	uh	flood	FLUHD
ĭ	i	pit	PIT	ûr	er	bird	BERD
ĭ (at end of a syllable)	ih	guitar	gih•TAR	z	z	xylophone	ZY•luh•fohn
ī	y eye (only for a complete syllable)	pie island	PY EYE•luhnd	z	z	bags	BAGZ
îr	ir	hear	HIR	zh	zh	decision	dih•SIZH•uhn
j	j	germ	JERM	ə	uh	around broken focus	uh•ROWND BROH•kuhn FOH•kuhs
k	k	kick	KIK	ər	er	winner	WIN•er
ng	ng	thing	THING	th	th	thin they	THIN THAY
ngk	ngk	bank	BANGK	w	w	one	WUHN
				wh	hw	whether	HWFTH•er

asteroid (AS•tuh•royd)
a small, rocky object that orbits the sun; most asteroids are located in a band between the orbits of Mars and Jupiter (93)
asteroide un objeto pequeño y rocoso que se encuentra en órbita alrededor del Sol; la mayoría de los asteroides se ubican en una banda entre las órbitas de Marte y Júpiter

astronomical unit (as•truh•NAHM•ih•kuhl YOO•nit)
the average distance between Earth and the sun; approximately 150 million kilometers (symbol, AU) (96)
unidad astronómica la distancia promedio entre la Tierra y el Sol; aproximadamente 150 millones de kilómetros (símbolo: UA)

comet (KAHM•it)
a small body of ice, rock, and cosmic dust that follows an elliptical orbit around the sun and that gives off gas and dust in the form of a tail as it passes close to the sun (93)
cometa un cuerpo pequeño formado por hielo, roca y polvo cósmico que sigue una órbita elíptica alrededor del Sol y que libera gas y polvo, los cuales forman una cola al pasar cerca del Sol

eclipse (ih•KLIPS)
an event in which the shadow of one celestial body falls on another (17)
eclipse un suceso en el que la sombra de un cuerpo celeste cubre otro cuerpo celeste

galaxy (GAL•uhk•see)
a collection of stars, dust, and gas bound together by gravity (106)
galaxia un conjunto de estrellas, polvo y gas unidos por la gravedad

gravity (GRAV•ih•tee)
a force of attraction between objects that is due to their masses (125)
gravedad una fuerza de atracción entre dos objetos debido a sus masas

light-year (LYT•yir)
the distance that light travels in one year; about 9.46 trillion kilometers (114)
año luz la distancia que viaja la luz en un año; aproximadamente 9.46 billones de kilómetros

orbit (OHR•bit)
the path that a body follows as it travels around another body in space (10, 134)
órbita la trayectoria que sigue un cuerpo al desplazarse alrededor de otro cuerpo en el espacio

parallax (PAIR•uh•laks)
an apparent shift in the position of an object when viewed from different locations (87)
paralaje un cambio aparente en la posición de un objeto cuando se ve desde lugares distintos

phase (FAYZ)
in astronomy, the change in the sunlit area of one celestial body as seen from another celestial body; phases of the moon are caused by the changing positions of Earth, the sun, and the moon (12)
fase en astronomía, el cambio que ocurre en el área de un cuerpo celeste que está iluminada por el Sol, tal como se ve desde otro cuerpo celeste; las fases de la Luna se producen por el cambio en la posición de la Tierra, el Sol y la Luna

protoplanetary disk (proh•toh•PLAN•ih•tehr•ee DISK)
a disk of gas and dust orbiting a newly formed star, from which planets may eventually form (68)
disco protoplanetario disco compuesto de gas y polvo que orbita alrededor de una estrella recién formada y del cual, con el tiempo, pueden surgir planetas

season (SEE•zuhn)
a division of the year that is characterized by recurring weather conditions and determined by both Earth's tilt relative to the sun and Earth's position in its orbit around the sun (33)
estación una de las partes en que se divide el año que se caracteriza por condiciones climáticas recurrentes y que está determinada tanto por la inclinación de la Tierra con relación al Sol como por la posición que ocupa en su órbita alrededor del Sol

solar nebula (SOH•ler NEB•yuh•luh)
a rotating cloud of gas and dust from which the sun and planets formed (67)
nebulosa solar una nube de gas y polvo en rotación a partir de la cual se formaron el Sol y los planetas

telescope (TEL•ih•skohp)
an instrument that collects light or other electromagnetic radiation from distant objects and concentrates it to make the objects appear larger or brighter (91)
telescopio instrumento que reúne luz u otra radiación electromegnética proveniente de objetos distantes y la concentra para que los objetos se vean más grandes o más brillantes

universe (YOO•nuh•vers)
space and all the matter and energy in it (106)
universo el espacio y toda la materia y energía que hay dentro de él

Index

Note: Italic page numbers represent illustrative material, such as figures, tables, margin elements, photographs, and illustrations. Boldface page numbers represent page numbers for definitions.

L

land of the midnight sun, 45–46
Language SmArts, 14, 37, 111, 134
   Organize Information Graphically,
      85, *85*
   Write an Origin Story, 73
Laplace, Pierre-Simon, 68
latitude, 37, *37*
law of universal gravitation, 125,
   141
laws of motion, 122–124, 141
Leap Year, 50
Leavitt, Henrietta, 113, 116
Lesson Self-Check, 25–27, 47–49,
   79–81, 101–103, 119–121,
   141–143
life cycle of stars, 74
Life Science Connection
   Growing Seasons in Different
      Regions, 50
light sources, 110–111, *110, 111*
light-year, 114
location
   determining within a field of
      objects, 108
long-distance space travel ship, *126*
Low Earth Orbit (LEO), 134
lunar eclipse, 17, *17*, 20
   partial lunar eclipse, 21
   penumbral lunar eclipse, 21
   timing of, 22, *22*
   total lunar eclipse, 21
lunar landing, 149

M

Mariner 4 probe, 66
Mars
   composition of, 75
   density of, *76*
   distance from the sun, 65
   as inner (terrestrial) planet, 64
   motion of, 125
   in night sky, *62, 64*, 85
   position in solar system, *63*
   visibility of, 57

mass
   of celestial objects, 136
   of Earth, 136
   gravitational field related to, 63, 128
   of the sun, 136
Math Connection
   Leap Year, 50
mathematical formulas, 99
mathematical models, 92, 100, 103
matter
   in the solar system, 136, *136*, 137
   in universe, 136
measurement
   of distance in space using
      brightness, 112
   of Milky Way, 114
   of solar system, 65
   value of measuring distances
      between celestial objects, 111
Mercury
   composition of, 75
   density of, *76*
   distance from the sun, *65*
   as inner (terrestrial) planet, 64
   lack of moons, 65
   in night sky, *64*, 85
   objects orbiting, *94*
   orbit of, *94*
   position in solar system, *63, 65*
   shape of, *94*
meteor, 65, 93, *93*
meteorites, 89, *89*
meteoroid, 65, 76, 92, 93, *93*
Milky Way, 57, *57, 105, 119, 123, 121*
   Earth's place in, 109
   modeling, 106–107
   motion within, 134
   role of gravity in, 133
   scale of, 115
   size of, 114
   stars and planets in, 115
models/modeling
   apparent motion of the sun, 8–9
   data that does not fit, 89
   Earth-Moon-Sun system, 55–56
   of Earth-sun relationship, 39–38
   exploring the solar system with,
      95–98

   of formation of solar system, 71
   gravity, 125–128
   mathematical models, 92
   Milky Way, 104–105
   museum model, 59
   nebular disk formation, 69–70
   scale of, 103
   scales in the universe, 114–116
   solar and lunar eclipses, 18–19
   of solar system, 66–68, 86–90, *86,*
      90, 95–98, *95, 102*, 103
   of solar system formation, 73
   sunlight distribution, 35
moon of Earth, 12–16, *12, 92, 116, 121*
   eclipse of, 20, *21*
   formation of, *146*
   Harvest Moon, 4
   light source, 12
   orbit of, 10, *10*, 11, 14, *15*, 22, *22*
   path of, 7, *7*, 10, *10*, 86
   phases of, 12–16, *12, 15*, 22, 26, 27,
      27, 84
   rotation of, 10, *10, 12*, 14
   as satellite, 132
   shaping of, 129
   solar eclipse and, 1, 19–20, *19, 20*
   surface of, 91
   visibility of, 5, 7
moons of planets
   composition of, 65
   formation of, *146*
   of gas planets, 75
   orbits of, 94
   position of Jupiter's moons, 91, *91*
   shape of, 93, *93*, 94
   shaping of, 129
motion/movement
   beyond our solar system, 135, *135*
   of celestial objects, 111
   circular motion, 126
   of constellations, 84, *84*
   of Earth's moon, 7, *7*, 10, *10*, 27, 86
   Earth's rotation and revolution,
      9–10, *9, 10*, 11, *11*, 42, *42, 47*
   of falling objects, 130–131
   of galaxies, 120
   within Milky Way, 134

What goes up comes down

Gravity has a pull down on everything

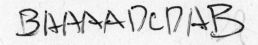

BAAADCDAB

what goes up comes down

Gravity has a Pull down on everything

SENTENCE STRUCTURE

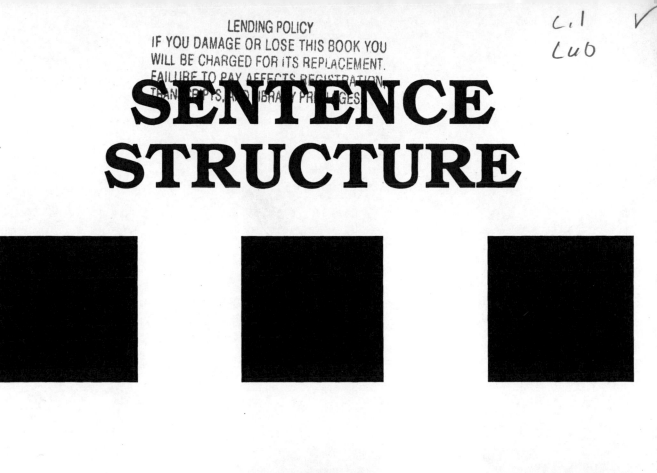

LINDELL R. BRUCE
LAS POSITAS COLLEGE

 KENDALL/HUNT PUBLISHING COMPANY
4050 Westmark Drive   Dubuque, Iowa 52002

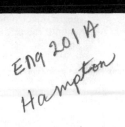

10

CONTENTS